diabetic
Holiday
recipes

Publications International, Ltd.

Favorite Brand Name Recipes is a trademark of Publications International, Ltd.

Pictured on the front cover *(clockwise from top):* Cranberry Phyllo Cheesecake Tart *(page 128),* Seared Beef Tenderloin with Horseradish-Rosemary Cream *(page 64),* Mini Smoked Salmon Latkes *(page 10)* and Herb-Roasted Chicken and Corn Bread Dressing *(page 54).*

Pictured on the back cover *(top to bottom):* Flourless Chocolate Cake *(page 134)* and Pork with Spicy Orange Cranberry Sauce *(page 66).*

ISBN-13: 978-1-60553-705-4
ISBN-10: 1-60553-705-5

Library of Congress Control Number: 2010921102

Manufactured in China.

8 7 6 5 4 3 2 1

Nutritional Analysis: Every effort has been made to check the accuracy of the nutritional information that appears with each recipe. However, because numerous variables account for a wide range of values for certain foods, nutritive analyses in this book should be considered approximate. Different results may be obtained by using different nutrient databases and different brand-name products.

Microwave Cooking: Microwave ovens vary in wattage. Use the cooking times as guidelines and check for doneness before adding more time.

Note: This book is for informational purposes and is not intended to provide medical advice. Neither Publications International, Ltd., nor the authors, editors or publisher takes responsibility for any possible consequences from any treatment, procedure, exercise, dietary modification, action, or applications of medication or preparation by any person reading or following the information in this cookbook. The publication of this book does not constitute the practice of medicine, and this cookbook does not replace your physician, pharmacist or health-care specialist. **Before undertaking any course of treatment or nutritional plan, the authors, editors and publisher advise the reader to check with a physician or other health-care provider.**

Not all recipes in this cookbook are appropriate for all people with diabetes. Health-care providers, registered dietitians and certified diabetes educators can help design specific meal plans tailored to individual needs.

Publications International, Ltd.

Contents

Bacon & Onion Cheese Ball

1 package (8 ounces) fat-free cream cheese, softened
½ cup fat-free sour cream
½ cup bottled real bacon bits
½ cup chopped green onions
¼ cup (1 ounce) blue cheese crumbles
   Additional sliced green onion (optional)
   Celery sticks or whole wheat crackers (optional)

1. Combine cream cheese, sour cream, bacon bits, green onions and blue cheese in medium bowl until well blended.

2. Shape mixture into a ball. Wrap in plastic wrap; refrigerate at least 1 hour before serving. Garnish with additional green onion; serve with celery or crackers, if desired.   *Makes 20 servings*

Nutrients per Serving: 2 tablespoons
Calories: 34, **Calories from Fat:** 35%, **Total Fat:** 1g, **Saturated Fat:** <1g,
Cholesterol: 7mg, **Sodium:** 203mg, **Carbohydrate:** 2g, **Fiber:** <1g, **Protein:** 4g

Dietary Exchanges: ½ Meat

Bacon & Onion Cheese Ball

Turkey Meatballs in Cranberry Barbecue Sauce

1 can (16 ounces) jellied cranberry sauce
½ cup barbecue sauce
1 egg white
1 pound 93% lean ground turkey
1 green onion, sliced
2 teaspoons grated orange peel
1 teaspoon reduced-sodium soy sauce
¼ teaspoon black pepper
⅛ teaspoon ground red pepper (optional)

Slow Cooker Directions

1. Combine cranberry sauce and barbecue sauce in slow cooker. Cover; cook on HIGH 20 to 30 minutes or until cranberry sauce is melted and mixture is hot.

2. Meanwhile, lightly beat egg white in medium bowl. Add turkey, green onion, orange peel, soy sauce, black pepper and ground red pepper, if desired; mix until well blended. Shape into 24 balls.

3. Spray large nonstick skillet with nonstick cooking spray. Add meatballs to skillet; cook over medium heat 8 to 10 minutes or until meatballs are cooked through, turning occasionally to brown evenly. Add to heated sauce in slow cooker; stir gently to coat.

4. *Reduce heat to LOW.* Cover; cook 3 hours. Transfer meatballs to serving bowl. *Makes 12 servings*

Nutrients per Serving: 2 meatballs with 2 tablespoons sauce
Calories: 137, **Calories from Fat:** 27%, **Total Fat:** 4g, **Saturated Fat:** 1g, **Cholesterol:** 19mg, **Sodium:** 206mg, **Carbohydrate:** 18g, **Fiber:** 1g, **Protein:** 7g

Dietary Exchanges: 1 Fruit, 1 Meat, ½ Fat

Turkey Meatballs in Cranberry Barbecue Sauce

Beefy Stuffed Mushrooms

1 pound 90% lean ground beef
2 teaspoons prepared horseradish
1 teaspoon chopped fresh chives
1 clove garlic, minced
¼ teaspoon black pepper
18 large mushrooms
⅔ cup dry white wine

1. Preheat oven to 350°F. Combine beef, horseradish, chives, garlic and pepper in medium bowl; mix well.

2. Remove stems from mushrooms; fill caps with beef mixture.

3. Place stuffed mushrooms in shallow baking dish; pour wine over mushrooms. Bake 20 minutes or until meat is cooked through.

Makes 18 servings

Nutrients per Serving: 1 mushroom
Calories: 40, **Calories from Fat:** 23%, **Total Fat:** 1g, **Saturated Fat:** 0g, **Cholesterol:** 13mg, **Sodium:** 20mg, **Carbohydrate:** 1g, **Fiber:** 0g, **Protein:** 6g

Dietary Exchanges: 1 Lean Meat

To clean mushrooms, wipe them with a damp paper towel, brush with a mushroom brush or rinse briefly under cold running water to remove the dirt. Pat dry before using, and trim and discard the stem ends. Never soak mushrooms in water because they absorb water and will become mushy.

Beefy Stuffed Mushrooms

Mini Smoked Salmon Latkes

2 cups frozen shredded hash brown potatoes, thawed and drained
1 egg, lightly beaten
2 tablespoons finely chopped shallot
1 tablespoon all-purpose flour
1 tablespoon whipping cream
½ teaspoon salt
¼ teaspoon black pepper
1 tablespoon butter
1 tablespoon vegetable oil
1 package (4 ounces) smoked salmon, cut into 24 pieces
  Fat-free sour cream (optional)
  Black whitefish caviar (optional)

1. Chop potatoes into smaller pieces. Combine potatoes, egg, shallot, flour, cream, salt and pepper in large bowl; mix well.

2. Heat half each of butter and oil in large nonstick skillet over medium-high heat. Spoon tablespoonfuls of potato mixture into skillet; flatten with spatula to make small pancakes. Cook about 3 minutes on each side or until browned. Remove to plate. Repeat with remaining butter, oil and potato mixture.

3. Top each pancake with smoked salmon, sour cream and caviar, if desired. Serve immediately. *Makes about 24 servings*

Nutrients per Serving: 1 latke
Calories: 35, **Calories from Fat:** 50%, **Total Fat:** 2g, **Saturated Fat:** 0g, **Cholesterol:** 12 mg, **Sodium:** 95mg, **Carbohydrate:** 4g, **Fiber:** 0g, **Protein:** 2g

Dietary Exchanges: ½ Vegetable, ½ Fat

Mini Smoked Salmon Latkes

Two-Tomato Kalamata Crostini

    8 sun-dried tomatoes (not packed in oil)
    1 baguette (4 ounces), cut into 20 (¼-inch-thick) slices
    5 ounces grape tomatoes, chopped
   12 kalamata olives, pitted and finely chopped
    2 teaspoons cider vinegar
 1½ teaspoons dried basil
    1 teaspoon extra virgin olive oil
   ⅛ teaspoon salt
    1 clove garlic, halved

1. Preheat oven to 350°F. Place sun-dried tomatoes in small bowl; cover with boiling water. Let stand 10 minutes. Drain tomatoes; cut into thin slices with serrated knife.

2. Place bread slices on large baking sheet. Bake 10 minutes or until golden brown around edges. Cool on wire rack.

3. Meanwhile, combine sun-dried tomatoes, grape tomatoes, olives, vinegar, basil, oil and salt in medium bowl; mix well.

4. Rub bread slices with garlic. Top each bread slice with 1 tablespoon tomato mixture.   *Makes 20 servings*

Nutrients per Serving: 1 crostino
Calories: 45, **Calories from Fat:** 24%, **Total Fat:** 1g, **Saturated Fat:** <1g,
Cholesterol: 0mg, **Sodium:** 219mg, **Carbohydrate:** 8g, **Fiber:** 1g, **Protein:** 1g

Dietary Exchanges: ½ Starch, ½ Fat

Two-Tomato Kalamata Crostini

Salmon and Crab Cakes

½ pound cooked salmon
½ pound cooked crabmeat*
1 egg, lightly beaten *or* ¼ cup cholesterol-free egg substitute
1½ tablespoons reduced-fat mayonnaise
1 tablespoon minced fresh parsley
1 teaspoon dried dill weed
½ teaspoon salt substitute
½ teaspoon black pepper
½ teaspoon Dijon mustard
¼ teaspoon reduced-sodium Worcestershire sauce
¼ cup plain dry bread crumbs

Lump crabmeat works best.

1. Flake salmon and crabmeat into medium bowl. Add egg, mayonnaise, parsley, dill, salt substitute, pepper, mustard and Worcestershire sauce; stir until well blended.

2. Place bread crumbs in shallow dish. Drop heaping ⅓ cup salmon mixture into bread crumbs; shape into thick patty. Repeat with remaining mixture.

3. Spray large nonstick skillet with nonstick cooking spray. Cook salmon and crab cakes, covered, over medium heat 5 to 8 minutes or until browned, turning once. *Makes 4 servings*

Nutrients per Serving: 1 cake
Calories: 251, **Calories from Fat:** 44%, **Total Fat:** 12g, **Saturated Fat:** 3g, **Cholesterol:** 130mg, **Sodium:** 379mg, **Carbohydrate:** 6g, **Fiber:** <1g, **Protein:** 29g

Dietary Exchanges: 4 Meat, 2 Fat

Salmon and Crab Cakes

Mini Marinated Beef Skewers

1 beef top round steak (about 1 pound)
2 tablespoons reduced-sodium soy sauce
1 tablespoon dry sherry
1 teaspoon dark sesame oil
2 cloves garlic, minced

1. Cut beef crosswise into 18 (⅛-inch-thick) slices. Place in large resealable food storage bag. Combine soy sauce, sherry, oil and garlic in small cup; pour over beef. Seal bag; turn to coat. Marinate in refrigerator at least 30 minutes or up to 2 hours.

2. Meanwhile, soak 18 (6-inch) wooden skewers in water 20 minutes.

3. Preheat broiler. Drain beef; discard marinade. Weave beef accordion-style onto skewers. Place on rack of broiler pan.

4. Broil 4 to 5 inches from heat 2 minutes. Turn skewers over; broil 2 minutes more or until beef is barely pink. Serve warm.

Makes 6 servings

Nutrients per Serving: 3 skewers
Calories: 120, **Calories from Fat:** 30%, **Total Fat:** 4g, **Saturated Fat:** 1g, **Cholesterol:** 60mg, **Sodium:** 99mg, **Carbohydrate:** 2g, **Fiber:** <1g, **Protein:** 20g

Dietary Exchanges: 2 Meat

Mini Marinated Beef Skewers

Spinach, Crab and Artichoke Dip

1 package (10 ounces) frozen chopped spinach, thawed
  and squeezed nearly dry
1 package (8 ounces) reduced-fat cream cheese
1 jar (about 6 ounces) marinated artichoke hearts, drained
  and finely chopped
1 can (6½ ounces) crabmeat, drained and shredded
¼ teaspoon hot pepper sauce
  Melba toast or whole grain crackers (optional)

Slow Cooker Directions

Combine spinach, cream cheese, artichokes, crabmeat and hot pepper
sauce in 1½-quart slow cooker. Cover; cook on HIGH 1½ to 2 hours
or until heated through, stirring after 1 hour. (Dip will stay warm in
slow cooker for 2 hours.) Serve with melba toast, if desired.

Makes 10 servings

Nutrients per Serving: ¼ cup dip
Calories: 99, **Calories from Fat:** 63%, **Total Fat:** 7g, **Saturated Fat:** 3g,
Cholesterol: 29mg, **Sodium:** 295mg, **Carbohydrate:** 3g, **Fiber:** 1g, **Protein:** 6g

Dietary Exchanges: 1 Vegetable, 1½ Fat

*Squeezing spinach dry is always a dreaded task.
To make it easier, be sure to thaw it first, then try pressing
the spinach between two plates or bowls (over the sink)
or putting it in a potato ricer.*

Spinach, Crab and Artichoke Dip

Spicy Polenta Cheese Bites

3 cups water
1 cup corn grits or cornmeal
½ teaspoon salt
¼ teaspoon chili powder
1 tablespoon butter
¼ cup minced onion or shallot
1 tablespoon minced jalapeño pepper*
½ cup (2 ounces) shredded sharp Cheddar cheese or fontina cheese

*Jalapeño peppers can sting and irritate the skin, so wear rubber gloves when handling peppers and do not touch your eyes.

1. Grease 8-inch square baking pan. Bring water to a boil in large nonstick saucepan over high heat. Slowly add grits, stirring constantly. Reduce heat to low; cook and stir until grits are tender and water is absorbed. Stir in salt and chili powder.

2. Melt butter in small saucepan over medium-high heat. Add onion and jalapeño; cook and stir 3 to 5 minutes or until tender. Stir into grits; mix well. Spread in prepared pan. Let stand 1 hour or until cool and firm.

3. Preheat broiler. Cut polenta into 16 squares. Arrange squares on nonstick baking sheet; sprinkle with Cheddar. Broil 4 inches from heat 5 minutes or until Cheddar is melted and slightly browned. Cut squares in half. Serve warm or at room temperature.   *Makes 16 servings*

Tip: For even spicier flavor, add ⅛ to ¼ teaspoon red pepper flakes to the onion-jalapeño mixture.

Nutrients per Serving: 2 pieces
Calories: 58, Calories from Fat: 32%, Total Fat: 2g, Saturated Fat: 1g, Cholesterol: 6mg, Sodium: 96mg, Carbohydrate: 8g, Fiber: 1g, Protein: 2g

Dietary Exchanges: ½ Starch, ½ Fat

Spicy Polenta Cheese Bites

Marinated Citrus Shrimp

1 pound (about 32) large raw shrimp, peeled and deveined
    (with tails on), cooked
2 oranges, peeled and cut into segments
1 can (5½ ounces) pineapple chunks in juice, drained and ¼ cup juice
    reserved
2 green onions, sliced
½ cup orange juice
2 tablespoons minced fresh cilantro
2 tablespoons lime juice
2 tablespoons white wine vinegar
1 tablespoon olive or vegetable oil
1 clove garlic, minced
½ teaspoon dried basil
½ teaspoon dried tarragon
    White pepper (optional)

1. Combine shrimp, orange segments, pineapple chunks and green onions in resealable food storage bag.

2. Mix orange juice, reserved pineapple juice, cilantro, lime juice, vinegar, oil, garlic, basil and tarragon in medium bowl; pour over shrimp mixture, turning to coat. Season to taste with white pepper, if desired. Marinate in refrigerator 2 hours or up to 8 hours.

3. Spoon shrimp mixture onto plates. *Makes 16 servings*

Nutrients per Serving: 2 shrimp
Calories: 51, **Calories from Fat:** 20%, **Total Fat:** 1g, **Saturated Fat:** <1g,
Cholesterol: 44mg, **Sodium:** 50mg, **Carbohydrate:** 5g, **Fiber:** 1g, **Protein:** 5g

Dietary Exchanges: ½ Fruit, ½ Meat

Marinated Citrus Shrimp

Cold Asparagus with Lemon-Mustard Dressing

      12 fresh asparagus spears
       2 tablespoons fat-free mayonnaise
       1 tablespoon sweet brown mustard
       1 tablespoon fresh lemon juice
       1 teaspoon grated lemon peel, divided

1. Steam asparagus until crisp-tender and bright green; immediately drain and rinse under cold water. Cover and refrigerate until chilled.

2. Combine mayonnaise, mustard, lemon juice and ½ teaspoon lemon peel in small bowl; mix well.

3. Divide asparagus between 2 plates. Spoon 2 tablespoons dressing over each serving; sprinkle each with remaining ¼ teaspoon lemon peel.   *Makes 2 servings*

Nutrients per Serving: 6 asparagus spears with 2 tablespoons dressing
Calories: 39, **Calories from Fat:** 14%, **Total Fat:** 1g, **Saturated Fat:** <1g, **Cholesterol:** 0mg, **Sodium:** 294mg, **Carbohydrate:** 7g, **Fiber:** 2g, **Protein:** 3g

Dietary Exchanges: 1½ Vegetable

Smoked Salmon Roses

       1 package (8 ounces) cream cheese, softened
       1 tablespoon prepared horseradish
       1 tablespoon minced fresh dill
       1 tablespoon half-and-half
      16 slices (12 to 16 ounces) smoked salmon
       1 red bell pepper, cut into thin strips
         Fresh dill sprigs

1. Beat cream cheese, horseradish, minced dill and half-and-half in medium bowl until light and creamy.

2. Spread 1 tablespoon cream cheese mixture over each salmon slice; roll up jelly-roll style. Cut each roll in half crosswise. Arrange salmon rolls on serving dish to resemble roses. Arrange bell pepper strips and dill sprig in center of each rose. *Makes 32 servings*

Nutrients per Serving: 1 appetizer
Calories: 40, **Calories from Fat:** 67%, **Total Fat:** 3g, **Saturated Fat:** 2g, **Cholesterol:** 10mg, **Sodium:** 106mg, **Carbohydrate:** 1g, **Fiber:** <1g, **Protein:** 3g

Dietary Exchanges: 1 Fat

Bacon & Cheese Dip

2 packages (8 ounces each) reduced-fat cream cheese, softened and cut into cubes
4 cups (16 ounces) shredded reduced-fat sharp Cheddar cheese
1 cup evaporated fat-free milk
2 tablespoons yellow mustard
1 tablespoon chopped onion
2 teaspoons Worcestershire sauce
½ teaspoon salt
¼ teaspoon hot pepper sauce (optional)
1 pound turkey bacon, crisp-cooked and crumbled
Vegetable dippers or crusty bread (optional)

Slow Cooker Directions

1. Combine cream cheese, Cheddar cheese, evaporated milk, mustard, onion, Worcestershire sauce, salt and hot pepper sauce, if desired, in slow cooker. Cover; cook on LOW 1 hour or until cheese melts, stirring occasionally.

2. Stir in bacon; adjust seasonings as desired. Serve with vegetables or bread, if desired. *Makes 32 servings (about 4 cups dip)*

Nutrients per Serving: 2 tablespoons dip
Calories: 114, **Calories from Fat:** 64%, **Total Fat:** 8g, **Saturated Fat:** 4g, **Cholesterol:** 27mg, **Sodium:** 436mg, **Carbohydrate:** 2g, **Fiber:** <1g, **Protein:** 7g

Dietary Exchanges: 1 Meat, 1 Fat

Butternut Squash Soup

2 teaspoons olive oil
1 large sweet onion, chopped
1 medium red bell pepper, chopped
2 packages (10 ounces each) frozen puréed butternut squash, thawed
1 can (10¾ ounces) condensed reduced-sodium chicken broth, undiluted
¼ teaspoon ground nutmeg
⅛ teaspoon white pepper
½ cup fat-free half-and-half

1. Heat oil in large saucepan over medium-high heat. Add onion and bell pepper; cook 5 minutes, stirring occasionally. Add squash, broth, nutmeg and white pepper; bring to a boil over high heat. Reduce heat; cover and simmer about 15 minutes or until vegetables are very tender.

2. Purée soup in saucepan with hand-held immersion blender or in batches in food processor or blender. Return soup to saucepan.

3. Stir in half-and-half; heat through. Add additional half-and-half, if necessary, to thin soup to desired consistency.   *Makes 4 servings*

Serving Suggestion: Garnish with a swirl of fat-free half-and-half or a sprinkle of fresh parsley.

Note: Butternut squash is an excellent source of beta-carotene, as well as vitamin C, potassium and dietary fiber.

Nutrients per Serving: 1½ cups
Calories: 152, **Calories from Fat:** 17%, **Total Fat:** 3g, **Saturated Fat:** 1g,
Cholesterol: 13mg, **Sodium:** 155mg, **Carbohydrate:** 28g, **Fiber:** 3g, **Protein:** 6g

Dietary Exchanges: 2 Starch, ½ Fat

Butternut Squash Soup

Fresh Cranberry-Pineapple Salad

1 medium orange
1 cup fresh or thawed frozen cranberries
⅔ cup water
1 package (4-serving size) sugar-free raspberry-flavored gelatin
1 cup ice cubes
½ (8-ounce) can crushed pineapple in juice, drained

1. Grate orange peel into small bowl. Coarsely chop cranberries in blender or food processor.

2. Squeeze juice from orange into small saucepan; stir in water. Bring to a boil over high heat. Remove from heat; stir in gelatin until completely dissolved. Add ice cubes; stir until gelatin is slightly thickened. Remove any unmelted ice.

3. Stir in cranberries, pineapple and orange peel; mix well. Pour into 4 (6-ounce) dishes or 9-inch pie plate. Cover and refrigerate until firm.

Makes 4 servings

Nutrients per Serving: ½ cup
Calories: 59, **Calories from Fat:** 2%, **Total Fat:** <1g, **Saturated Fat:** <1g,
Cholesterol: 0mg, **Sodium:** 56mg, **Carbohydrate:** 13g, **Fiber:** 2g, **Protein:** 2g

Dietary Exchanges: 1 Fruit

Fresh cranberries are readily available September through December. Since they are not available fresh during the rest of the year, buy a few extra bags for the freezer, where they will keep for up to one year.

Fresh Cranberry-Pineapple Salad

New England Clam Chowder

   4 ounces smoked turkey sausage, finely chopped
1½ cups chopped onions
2¾ cups fat-free (skim) milk
   1 medium red potato, diced
   1 can (6½ ounces) minced clams, drained, liquid reserved
   2 bay leaves
½ teaspoon dried thyme
   2 tablespoons reduced-fat margarine
¼ teaspoon black pepper
 15 reduced-sodium fat-free saltine crackers

1. Spray large saucepan or Dutch oven with nonstick cooking spray; heat over medium-high heat. Add sausage; cook and stir 2 minutes or until browned. Transfer to plate.

2. Spray saucepan with nonstick cooking spray. Add onions; cook and stir 2 minutes. Add milk, potato, reserved clam liquid, bay leaves and thyme; cover and simmer 15 minutes or until potato is tender.

3. Remove bay leaves. Stir in sausage, clams, margarine and pepper. Simmer until heated through, stirring frequently. Divide chowder among 5 bowls; crumble crackers over top.   *Makes 5 servings*

Nutrients per Serving: 1 cup
Calories: 269, **Calories from Fat:** 19%, **Total Fat:** 6g, **Saturated Fat:** 1g, **Cholesterol:** 42mg, **Sodium:** 468mg, **Carbohydrate:** 34g, **Fiber:** 2g, **Protein:** 20g

Dietary Exchanges: 2 Starch, 2 Meat

New England Clam Chowder

Roasted Vegetable Salad

2 cups sliced mushrooms
2 cups sliced carrots
2 cups chopped green or yellow bell peppers
2 cups cherry tomatoes, halved
1 cup chopped onion
¼ cup chopped pitted kalamata olives
4 teaspoons lemon juice, divided
2 teaspoons dried oregano
2 teaspoons olive oil
1 teaspoon black pepper
2 teaspoons sugar substitute (optional)
6 cups packed torn stemmed spinach or baby spinach

1. Preheat oven to 375°F. Combine mushrooms, carrots, bell peppers, tomatoes, onion and olives in large bowl. Add 2 teaspoons lemon juice, oregano, oil and black pepper; toss to coat.

2. Spread vegetables in single layer on two baking sheets. Roast 20 minutes, stirring once.

3. Stir in remaining 2 teaspoons lemon juice and sugar substitute, if desired. Serve warm over spinach.   *Makes 4 servings*

Nutrients per Serving:
Calories: 121, Calories from Fat: 29%, Total Fat: 4g, Saturated Fat: <1g, Cholesterol: 0mg, Sodium: 314mg, Carbohydrate: 20g, Fiber: 6g, Protein: 5g

Dietary Exchanges: 3 Vegetable, 1 Fat

Roasted Vegetable Salad

Easy Chicken, Spinach and Wild Rice Soup

1 can (about 14 ounces) reduced-sodium chicken broth
1¾ cups chopped carrots
2 cups cooked wild rice
2 cans (10¾ ounces each) condensed reduced-fat reduced-sodium cream of chicken soup, undiluted
1 teaspoon dried thyme
¼ teaspoon dried sage
¼ teaspoon black pepper
2 cups coarsely chopped baby spinach
1½ cups chopped cooked chicken*
½ cup fat-free half-and-half or fat-free (skim) milk

*Half of a rotisserie chicken will yield about 1½ cups of cooked meat.

1. Bring broth to a boil in large saucepan. Add carrots; cook 10 minutes.

2. Add rice, soup, thyme, sage and pepper to saucepan; bring to a boil. Stir in spinach, chicken and milk. Cook, stirring occasionally, about 2 minutes or until heated through.   *Makes 6 to 7 servings*

Nutrients per Serving: 1 cup
Calories: 256, **Calories from Fat:** 25%, **Total Fat:** 7g, **Saturated Fat:** 2g, **Cholesterol:** 62mg, **Sodium:** 624mg, **Carbohydrate:** 28g, **Fiber:** 3g, **Protein:** 22g

Dietary Exchanges: 2 Starch, 2 Meat

*Easy Chicken, Spinach
and Wild Rice Soup*

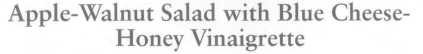
Apple-Walnut Salad with Blue Cheese-Honey Vinaigrette

¼ cup chopped walnuts
1 tablespoon white wine vinegar
2 teaspoons olive oil
2 teaspoons honey
¼ teaspoon salt
⅛ teaspoon black pepper
2 tablespoons crumbled blue cheese
1 large head Bibb lettuce, separated into leaves
1 small Red Delicious or other red apple, thinly sliced
1 small Granny Smith apple, thinly sliced

1. Place walnuts in small skillet; cook and stir over medium heat 5 minutes or until fragrant and lightly toasted. Transfer to plate to cool.

2. Whisk vinegar, oil, honey, salt and pepper in small bowl until well blended. Stir in cheese.

3. Divide lettuce and apples evenly among 4 plates. Drizzle dressing evenly over each salad; sprinkle with walnuts. *Makes 4 servings*

Nutrients per Serving:
Calories: 133, **Calories from Fat:** 37%, **Total Fat:** 6g, **Saturated Fat:** 1g, **Cholesterol:** 3mg, **Sodium:** 135mg, **Carbohydrate:** 20g, **Fiber:** 2g, **Protein:** 4g

Dietary Exchanges: 1 Vegetable, 1 Fruit, 1 Fat

Broccoli Cream Soup

1 tablespoon olive oil
2 cups chopped onions
1 pound fresh or frozen broccoli florets or spears
2 cups reduced-sodium chicken or vegetable broth
6 tablespoons cream cheese
1 cup milk
¾ teaspoon salt (optional)
⅛ teaspoon ground red pepper
⅓ cup finely chopped green onions

1. Heat oil in large saucepan over medium-high heat. Add onions; cook and stir 4 minutes or until translucent. Add broccoli and broth; bring to a boil over high heat. Reduce heat; cover and simmer 10 minutes or until broccoli is tender.

2. Working in batches, process mixture in food processor or blender until smooth. Return to saucepan; heat over medium heat.

3. Whisk in cream cheese until melted. Stir in milk, salt, if desired, and red pepper; cook 2 minutes or until heated through. Top with green onions. *Makes 5 servings*

Nutrients per Serving: 1 cup
Calories: 115, **Calories from Fat:** 24%, **Total Fat:** 4g, **Saturated Fat:** 2g,
Cholesterol: 10mg, **Sodium:** 569mg, **Carbohydrate:** 16g, **Fiber:** 4g, **Protein:** 7g

Dietary Exchanges: 1 Starch, 1 Meat

Spicy Pumpkin Soup with Green Chile Swirl

1 can (4 ounces) diced green chiles
¼ cup reduced-fat sour cream
¼ cup fresh cilantro
1 can (15 ounces) solid-pack pumpkin
1 can (about 14 ounces) fat-free reduced-sodium chicken or
    vegetable broth
½ cup water
1 teaspoon ground cumin
½ teaspoon chili powder
¼ teaspoon garlic powder
⅛ teaspoon ground red pepper (optional)
    Additional sour cream (optional)

1. Combine chiles, ¼ cup sour cream and cilantro in food processor or blender; process until smooth.*

2. Combine pumpkin, broth, water, cumin, chili powder, garlic powder and red pepper, if desired, in medium saucepan; stir in ¼ cup green chile mixture. Bring to a boil. Reduce heat to medium; simmer, uncovered, 5 minutes, stirring occasionally.

3. Pour into 4 serving bowls. Top each serving with small dollops of remaining green chile mixture and additional sour cream, if desired. Run tip of spoon through dollops to swirl.   *Makes 4 servings*

Omit food processor step by adding green chiles directly to soup. Finely chop cilantro and combine with sour cream. Dollop with sour cream-cilantro mixture as directed.

Nutrients per Serving:
Calories: 72, Calories from Fat: 17%, **Total Fat:** 1g, **Saturated Fat:** <1g, **Cholesterol:** 5mg, **Sodium:** 276mg, **Carbohydrate:** 12g, **Fiber:** 4g, **Protein:** 4g

Dietary Exchanges: 1 Starch

*Spicy Pumpkin Soup with
Green Chile Swirl*

Spinach Salad with Beets

6 cups packed baby spinach or torn spinach leaves (6 ounces)
1 cup canned pickled julienned beets, well drained
¼ cup thinly sliced red onion, separated into rings
¼ cup fat-free croutons
⅓ cup low-fat raspberry vinaigrette salad dressing
¼ cup real bacon bits
   Black pepper (optional)

1. Combine spinach, beets, onion and croutons in large bowl. Add dressing; toss to coat.

2. Divide evenly among 4 serving plates. Sprinkle with bacon bits and pepper, if desired. *Makes 4 servings*

Nutrients per Serving: 2 cups
Calories: 80, **Calories from Fat:** 34%, **Total Fat:** 3g, **Saturated Fat:** <1g, **Cholesterol:** 5mg, **Sodium:** 740mg, **Carbohydrate:** 9g, **Fiber:** 2g, **Protein:** 5g

Dietary Exchanges: 2 Vegetable, ½ Fat

Do not wash spinach before storing. Store loose spinach lightly packed in a plastic bag in the refrigerator. Leave prepackaged spinach in its original plastic bag; it will keep for three to four days.

Spinach Salad with Beets

Kale and White Bean Soup

  2 slices reduced-sodium bacon, chopped
½ cup diced onion
  1 unpeeled new red potato, diced
  2 cans (about 14 ounces each) reduced-sodium vegetable broth
  1 teaspoon minced garlic
½ teaspoon dried oregano
  2 bay leaves
  1 can (14½ ounces) low-sodium sliced carrots, drained
  1 can (13½ ounces) kale or spinach, drained
  1 can (10 ounces) reduced-sodium white kidney beans, rinsed and
      drained
⅓ cup finely chopped sun-dried tomatoes, packed in oil
  1 tablespoon olive oil
¼ teaspoon black pepper
⅛ teaspoon salt

1. Cook bacon in large saucepan over medium heat until crisp.
Drain fat.

2. Add onion and potato to saucepan; cook and stir 10 minutes or
until onion is browned. Stir in broth, garlic, oregano and bay leaves;
bring to a simmer. Cover and simmer 5 minutes or until potato is
tender.

3. Add carrots, kale, beans and sun-dried tomatoes; cook 5 minutes.
Remove bay leaves. Stir in oil, pepper and salt.   *Makes 6 servings*

Nutrients per Serving: 1 cup
Calories: 165, **Calories from Fat:** 27%, **Total Fat:** 5g, **Saturated Fat:** 1g,
Cholesterol: 2mg, **Sodium:** 479mg, **Carbohydrate:** 24g, **Fiber:** 6g, **Protein:** 7g

Dietary Exchanges: 2½ Starch, 1 Fat

Kale and White Bean Soup

Citrus Rice Salad

1 cup cooked brown rice, cooled to room temperature
1 stalk celery, chopped
1 medium seedless orange, peeled and cut into ½-inch pieces
1 tablespoon orange juice
1½ teaspoons canola oil
1½ teaspoons white wine vinegar
½ teaspoon curry powder
¼ teaspoon salt
⅛ teaspoon pepper
2 tablespoons minced fresh chives
2 tablespoons sliced almonds

1. Combine rice, celery and orange in medium serving bowl.

2. Whisk orange juice, oil, vinegar, curry powder, salt and pepper in small bowl until well blended.

3. Pour dressing over rice mixture; mix well. Stir in chives. Sprinkle with almonds just before serving. *Makes 4 servings*

Nutrients per Serving: ½ cup
Calories: 109, **Calories from Fat:** 33%, **Total Fat:** 4g, **Saturated Fat:** 0g, **Cholesterol:** 0mg, **Sodium:** 155mg, **Carbohydrate:** 17g, **Fiber:** 2g, **Protein:** 2g

Dietary Exchanges: 1 Starch, 1 Fat

Citrus Rice Salad

Mediterranean Fish Soup

4 ounces uncooked pastina or other small pasta
¾ cup chopped onion
2 cloves garlic, minced
1 teaspoon whole fennel seeds
1 can (about 14 ounces) no-salt-added stewed tomatoes
1 can (about 14 ounces) fat-free reduced-sodium chicken broth
1 tablespoon minced fresh Italian parsley
½ teaspoon black pepper
¼ teaspoon ground turmeric
8 ounces firm, white-fleshed fish, cut into 1-inch pieces
3 ounces small raw shrimp, peeled and deveined (with tails on)

1. Cook pasta according to package directions, omitting salt. Drain; keep warm.

2. Spray large nonstick saucepan with nonstick cooking spray; heat over medium heat. Add onion, garlic and fennel seeds; cook and stir 3 minutes or until onion is tender.

3. Stir in tomatoes, broth, parsley, pepper and turmeric. Bring to a boil; reduce heat and simmer 10 minutes. Add fish; cook 1 minute. Add shrimp; cook until shrimp are pink and opaque.

4. Divide pasta among 4 bowls; ladle soup over pasta.

Makes 4 servings

Nutrients per Serving: 1½ cups soup with ½ cup pasta
Calories: 209, **Calories from Fat:** 10%, **Total Fat:** 2g, **Saturated Fat:** <1g,
Cholesterol: 59mg, **Sodium:** 111mg, **Carbohydrate:** 28g, **Fiber:** 3g, **Protein:** 19g

Dietary Exchanges: 1½ Vegetable, 1½ Starch, 1½ Meat

Mediterranean Fish Soup

Greens and Pear with Maple-Mustard Dressing

¼ cup maple syrup
1 tablespoon Dijon mustard
1 tablespoon olive oil
1 tablespoon balsamic or cider vinegar
⅛ teaspoon black pepper
4 cups torn mixed salad greens
1 medium red pear, cored and thinly sliced
¼ cup sliced green onions
3 tablespoons dried cherries
2 tablespoons plus 2 teaspoons chopped walnuts, toasted*

To toast walnuts, place in small skillet; cook over medium heat 5 to 7 minutes or until fragrant, stirring occasionally.

1. Whisk syrup, mustard, oil, vinegar and pepper in small bowl until well blended.

2. Combine greens, pear, green onions, cherries and walnuts in large serving bowl. Drizzle with dressing; toss gently to coat.

Makes 4 servings

Nutrients per Serving:
Calories: 179, Calories from Fat: 34%, Total Fat: 7g, Saturated Fat: 1g, Cholesterol: 0mg, Sodium: 112mg, Carbohydrate: 29g, Fiber: 3g, Protein: 2g

Dietary Exchanges: 1 Vegetable, 1½ Fruit, 1 Fat

Greens and Pear with Maple-Mustard Dressing

Cranberry Chutney Glazed Salmon

½ teaspoon salt (optional)
½ teaspoon ground cinnamon
¼ teaspoon ground red pepper
 4 skinless salmon fillets (5 to 6 ounces each)
¼ cup cranberry chutney
 1 tablespoon white wine vinegar or cider vinegar

1. Preheat broiler or prepare grill for indirect cooking. Combine salt, if desired, cinnamon and red pepper in small cup; sprinkle over salmon.

2. Combine chutney and vinegar in small bowl; brush evenly over salmon fillets.

3. Broil 5 to 6 inches from heat source or grill over medium-hot coals on covered grill 4 to 6 minutes or until salmon is opaque in center.

Makes 4 servings

Variation: If cranberry chutney is not available, substitute mango chutney. Chop any large pieces of mango.

Nutrients per Serving: 1 salmon fillet
Calories: 229, **Calories from Fat:** 35%, **Total Fat:** 9g, **Saturated Fat:** 1g, **Cholesterol:** 78mg, **Sodium:** 104mg, **Carbohydrate:** 7g, **Fiber:** <1g, **Protein:** 28g

Dietary Exchanges: ½ Fruit, 4 Meat

Cranberry Chutney
Glazed Salmon

Holiday Beef Brisket

1 large onion, thinly sliced
1 small (2 to 2½ pounds) well-trimmed first-cut beef brisket
½ teaspoon salt
½ teaspoon black pepper
⅔ cups chili sauce, divided
1½ tablespoons packed brown sugar
¼ teaspoon ground cinnamon
2 large sweet potatoes, peeled and cut into 1-inch pieces
1 cup (5 ounces) pitted prunes (dried plums)
2 tablespoons cornstarch
2 tablespoons cold water

Slow Cooker Directions

1. Place onion in slow cooker. Arrange brisket over onion (tucking edges under to fit, if necessary). Sprinkle with salt and pepper; top with ⅓ cup chili sauce. Cover; cook on HIGH 3½ hours.

2. Combine remaining ⅓ cup chili sauce, brown sugar and cinnamon in large bowl. Add sweet potatoes and prunes; toss to coat. Spoon mixture over brisket. Cover; cook on HIGH 1¼ to 1½ hours or until brisket and sweet potatoes are tender.

3. Transfer brisket to cutting board; tent with foil. Transfer vegetables to serving platter, leaving juices in slow cooker. Keep vegetables warm.

4. Blend cornstarch into water in small cup until smooth. Stir mixture into slow cooker juices. Cover; cook on HIGH 10 minutes or until sauce thickens.

5. Cut brisket crosswise into thin slices. Arrange on serving platter with vegetables; top with sauce.   *Makes 8 servings*

Nutrients per Serving: 4 ounces brisket with ½ cup vegetables and ¼ cup sauce
Calories: 284, **Calories from Fat:** 22%, **Total Fat:** 7g, **Saturated Fat:** 2g,
Cholesterol: 68mg, **Sodium:** 523mg, **Carbohydrate:** 30g, **Fiber:** 4g, **Protein:** 25g

Dietary Exchanges: 2 Starch, 3 Meat

Holiday Beef Brisket

Herb-Roasted Chicken and Corn Bread Dressing

Chicken

- ½ cup chopped fresh parsley
- 2 tablespoons lemon juice
- 2 teaspoons grated lemon peel
- 1 teaspoon dried thyme
- ¾ teaspoon dried sage
- ½ teaspoon dried rosemary
- ½ teaspoon salt
- ¼ teaspoon black pepper
- 1 whole chicken (3½ to 4 pounds)
- 1 cup water

Dressing

- 4 ounces reduced-fat bulk breakfast sausage
- 1 cup finely chopped onion
- 2 medium stalks celery with leaves, thinly sliced
- 1 medium red bell pepper, diced
- 1 can (about 14 ounces) reduced-sodium chicken broth
- 2 cups corn bread stuffing mix
- ½ teaspoon poultry seasoning

1. Adjust oven rack to lowest position. Preheat oven to 450°F. Combine parsley, lemon juice, lemon peel, thyme, sage, rosemary, salt and pepper in small bowl; mix well.

2. Separate chicken skin from meat by sliding fingers under skin. Spread parsley mixture evenly under loosened skin. (If skin tears, use toothpicks to hold skin together.) Place on rack in roasting pan, breast side up.

3. Roast chicken 20 minutes. Add water to pan; roast 40 minutes or until meat thermometer inserted into thickest part of thigh registers 165°F. Tent with foil; let stand 15 minutes before slicing.

continued on page 56

Herb-Roasted Chicken and Corn Bread Dressing

Herb-Roasted Chicken and Corn Bread Dressing, continued

4. Meanwhile, spray large nonstick saucepan with nonstick cooking spray; heat over medium-high heat. Add sausage; cook 3 minutes or until browned, stirring to break up meat. Remove sausage from saucepan; drain fat.

5. Add onion, celery and bell pepper to saucepan; spray with cooking spray. Cook and stir over medium heat 7 minutes or until celery is tender. Stir in broth; bring to a boil. Remove from heat. Add sausage, stuffing mix and poultry seasoning; mix well. Serve with chicken.

Makes 6 servings

Tip: To reduce calories, fat and saturated fat, remove and discard the chicken skin before serving. This will reduce calories to about 270, fat grams to about 9 and saturated fat to about 2 grams per serving.

Nutrients per Serving: 3 ounces chicken with ¾ cup dressing
Calories: 280, **Calories from Fat:** 32%, **Total Fat:** 10g, **Saturated Fat:** 3g,
Cholesterol: 195mg, **Sodium:** 576mg, **Carbohydrate:** 11g, **Fiber:** 1g, **Protein:** 31g

Dietary Exchanges: 1 Starch, 3 Meat, 1½ Fat

Rosemary Roast Pork Tenderloin and Vegetables

¼ cup reduced-sodium chicken broth
1 tablespoon olive or vegetable oil
3 large parsnips, peeled and cut diagonally into ½-inch slices
2 cups baby carrots
1 red bell pepper, cut into ¾-inch pieces
1 medium sweet or yellow onion, cut into wedges
2 small pork tenderloins (12 ounces each)
2 tablespoons Dijon or spicy Dijon mustard
2 teaspoons dried rosemary
¾ teaspoon salt (optional)
½ teaspoon black pepper

1. Preheat oven to 400°F. Spray large shallow roasting pan or jelly-roll pan with nonstick cooking spray.

2. Combine broth and oil in small bowl. Combine parsnips, carrots and 3 tablespoons broth mixture in prepared pan; toss to coat. Roast vegetables 10 minutes.

3. Add bell pepper, onion and remaining broth mixture to pan; toss to coat. Push vegetables to edges of pan. Place pork in center; spread with mustard. Sprinkle pork and vegetables with rosemary, salt, if desired, and black pepper.

4. Roast 25 to 30 minutes or until vegetables are tender and meat thermometer inserted into center of tenderloin registers 155°F. Transfer pork to cutting board. Tent with foil; let stand 5 minutes. Cut pork crosswise into ½-inch slices; serve with vegetables and any juices from pan. *Makes 6 servings*

Nutrients per Serving: 3 ounces pork with ⅔ cup vegetables
Calories: 218, **Calories from Fat:** 25%, **Total Fat:** 6g, **Saturated Fat:** 2g, **Cholesterol:** 73mg, **Sodium:** 202mg, **Carbohydrate:** 14g, **Fiber:** 3g, **Protein:** 25g

Dietary Exchanges: 1 Starch, 3 Meat

Pork tenderloin is exactly what it sound like: the most tender cut of meat from the loin. It is a strip of meat that lies along each side of the backbone. Tenderloin is the leanest cut of pork and adapts well to a wide variety of flavors and cooking methods. Beside being versatile and delicious, lean pork is a terrific source of protein, B vitamins and zinc.

Fresh Garlic Shrimp Linguine

6 ounces multigrain linguine or spaghetti, broken in half
8 ounces frozen peeled and deveined shrimp
3 tablespoons diet margarine
½ teaspoon seafood seasoning
1 medium clove garlic, minced
¼ cup grated Parmesan cheese
¼ cup finely chopped fresh parsley (optional)
⅛ teaspoon salt (optional)

1. Cook linguine according to package directions, omitting salt, about 7 minutes or until al dente.

2. Add shrimp; cook 3 to 4 minutes or until shrimp are pink and opaque. Drain linguine and shrimp; tansfer to medium bowl.

3. Add margarine, seafood seasoning and garlic; toss gently to coat. Add Parmesan, parsley and salt, if desired; toss to combine.

Makes 4 servings

Nutrients per Serving: 1 cup
Calories: 270, **Calories from Fat:** 25%, **Total Fat:** 7g, **Saturated Fat:** 2g, **Cholesterol:** 91mg, **Sodium:** 242mg, **Carbohydrate:** 30g, **Fiber:** 3g, **Protein:** 21g

Dietary Exchanges: 2 Starch, 2 Meat

Fresh Garlic Shrimp Linguine

Chicken Piccata

   3 tablespoons all-purpose flour
½ teaspoon salt
¼ teaspoon black pepper
   4 boneless skinless chicken breasts (4 ounces each)
   2 teaspoons olive oil
   1 teaspoon butter
   2 cloves garlic, minced
¾ cup fat-free reduced-sodium chicken broth
   1 tablespoon fresh lemon juice
   2 tablespoons chopped fresh Italian parsley
   1 tablespoon capers, drained

1. Combine flour, salt and pepper in shallow dish. Reserve 1 tablespoon flour mixture.

2. Pound chicken to ½-inch thickness between sheets of waxed paper with flat side of meat mallet or rolling pin. Coat chicken with remaining flour mixture, shaking off excess.

3. Heat oil and butter in large nonstick skillet over medium heat. Add chicken; cook 4 to 5 minutes on each side or until no longer pink in center. Transfer to serving platter; cover loosely with foil.

4. Add garlic to same skillet; cook and stir 1 minute. Add reserved flour mixture; cook and stir 1 minute. Add broth and lemon juice; cook and stir 2 minutes or until thickened. Stir in parsley and capers; spoon sauce over chicken.

Makes 4 servings

Nutrients per Serving: 1 chicken breast with about ¼ cup sauce
Calories: 194, **Calories from Fat:** 30%, **Total Fat:** 6g, **Saturated Fat:** 2g,
Cholesterol: 71mg, **Sodium:** 473mg, **Carbohydrate:** 5g, **Fiber:** <1g, **Protein:** 27g

Dietary Exchanges: ½ Starch, 3 Meat

Chicken Piccata

Oven-Roasted Boston Scrod

½ cup seasoned dry bread crumbs
1 teaspoon grated lemon peel
1 teaspoon paprika
1 teaspoon dried dill weed
3 tablespoons all-purpose flour
2 egg whites
1 tablespoon water
1½ pounds Boston scrod fillets, cut into 6 pieces (about 4 ounces each)
2 tablespoons margarine, melted
Tartar Sauce (recipe follows)
Lemon wedges

1. Preheat oven to 400°F. Spray 15×10-inch jelly-roll pan with nonstick cooking spray. Combine bread crumbs, lemon peel, paprika and dill in shallow bowl or pie plate. Place flour in shallow dish. Beat egg whites and water in another shallow bowl or pie plate.

2. Add fish, 1 piece at a time, to flour; turn to coat lightly. Dip fish into egg white mixture, letting excess drip off, then roll in bread crumb mixture. Place on prepared pan; drizzle margarine evenly over fish.

3. Roast 15 to 18 minutes or until fish begins to flake when tested with fork.

4. Meanwhile, prepare Tartar Sauce. Serve fish with Tartar Sauce and lemon wedges. *Makes 6 servings*

Tartar Sauce: Combine ½ cup fat-free or reduced-fat mayonnaise, ¼ cup sweet pickle relish, 2 teaspoons Dijon mustard and ¼ teaspoon hot pepper sauce, if desired, in small bowl; mix well.

Nutrients per Serving: 1 piece scrod with 2 tablespoons sauce
Calories: 215, **Calories from Fat:** 21%, **Total Fat:** 5g, **Saturated Fat:** 1g, **Cholesterol:** 49mg, **Sodium:** 754mg, **Carbohydrate:** 18g, **Fiber:** <1g, **Protein:** 23g

Dietary Exchanges: 1 Starch, 2½ Meat

Oven-Roasted Boston Scrod

Seared Beef Tenderloin with Horseradish-Rosemary Cream

1 teaspoon chili powder
½ teaspoon salt, divided
¼ teaspoon plus ⅛ teaspoon black pepper, divided
1 pound beef tenderloin
1 clove garlic, halved
⅓ cup fat-free sour cream
3 tablespoons fat-free (skim) milk
2 teaspoons reduced-fat mayonnaise
1 teaspoon prepared horseradish
¼ teaspoon dried rosemary

1. Preheat oven to 425°F. Combine chili powder, ¼ teaspoon salt and ¼ teaspoon pepper in small bowl. Rub tenderloin with garlic; sprinkle evenly with seasoning mixture.

2. Heat medium ovenproof skillet over medium-high heat; spray with nonstick cooking spray. Cook tenderloin 2 minutes on each side.

3. Place skillet in oven. Roast 30 minutes or until meat thermometer inserted into thickest part of tenderloin registers 140°F. Tent with foil; let stand 15 minutes.

4. Meanwhile, combine sour cream, milk, mayonnaise, horseradish, rosemary, remaining ¼ teaspoon salt and ⅛ teaspoon pepper in small bowl; mix well. Cut tenderloin into 4 pieces; serve with sauce.

Makes 4 servings

Nutrients per Serving: 3 ounces beef with 2 tablespoons sauce
Calories: 205, **Calories from Fat:** 39%, **Total Fat:** 9g, **Saturated Fat:** 3g,
Cholesterol: 72mg, **Sodium:** 402mg, **Carbohydrate:** 5g, **Fiber:** <1g, **Protein:** 25g

Dietary Exchanges: ½ Starch, 3 Meat

Seared Beef Tenderloin with Horseradish-Rosemary Cream

Pork with Spicy Orange Cranberry Sauce

　1 teaspoon chili powder
　½ teaspoon ground cumin
　¼ teaspoon ground allspice
　¼ teaspoon salt
　¼ teaspoon black pepper
　4 boneless pork chops (about 1 pound)
　1 tablespoon canola oil
　1 cup whole-berry cranberry sauce
　½ teaspoon grated orange peel
　¼ teaspoon ground cinnamon
　⅛ teaspoon red pepper flakes

1. Combine chili powder, cumin, allspice, salt and black pepper in small bowl; mix well. Sprinkle evenly over both sides of pork chops.

2. Heat oil in large nonstick skillet over medium heat. Add pork; cook 4 to 5 minutes on each side or until barely pink in center.

3. Combine cranberry sauce, orange peel, cinnamon and red pepper flakes in small bowl; mix well. Serve sauce with pork chops.

Makes 4 servings

Nutrients per Serving: 1 pork chop with ¼ cup sauce
Calories: 276, **Calories from Fat:** 28%, **Total Fat:** 9g, **Saturated Fat:** 2g, **Cholesterol:** 51mg, **Sodium:** 204mg, **Carbohydrate:** 28g, **Fiber:** 2g, **Protein:** 20g

Dietary Exchanges: 2 Fruit, 3 Meat

*Pork with Spicy Orange
Cranberry Sauce*

Mustard, Garlic and Herb Roasted Turkey Breast

¼ cup spicy brown mustard
¼ cup chopped fresh parsley
 2 tablespoons chopped fresh thyme *or* 2 teaspoons dried thyme
 2 tablespoons chopped fresh sage *or* 2 teaspoons dried sage
 2 cloves garlic, minced
½ teaspoon black pepper
¼ teaspoon salt
 1 (6- to 7-pound) bone-in whole turkey breast

1. Preheat oven to 450°F. Combine mustard, parsley, thyme, sage, garlic, pepper and salt in medium bowl; mix well.

2. Loosen skin from turkey breast by inserting fingers and gently pushing between skin and meat. Rub mustard mixture under loosened skin, distributing mixture evenly over breast. Place turkey on rack in shallow roasting pan.

3. Place turkey in oven. *Immediately reduce oven temperature to 325°F.* Roast 2 to 2½ hours or until meat themometer inserted into thickest part of breast registers 165°F.

4. Transfer turkey to cutting board. Tent with foil; let stand 10 minutes before slicing. Remove skin; slice turkey.   *Makes 17 servings*

Nutrients per Serving: 3 ounces turkey
Calories: 128, **Calories from Fat:** 13%, **Total Fat:** 2g, **Saturated Fat:** <1g,
Cholesterol: 74mg, **Sodium:** 136mg, **Carbohydrate:** <1g, **Fiber:** <1g, **Protein:** 25g

Dietary Exchanges: 3 Meat

*Mustard, Garlic and Herb
Roasted Turkey Breast*

Lemon-Dijon Chicken with Potatoes

2 medium lemons
½ cup chopped fresh parsley
2 tablespoons Dijon mustard
4 cloves garlic, minced
2 teaspoons olive oil
1 teaspoon dried rosemary
¾ teaspoon black pepper
½ teaspoon salt
1 whole chicken (about 3½ pounds)
1½ pounds small red potatoes, cut into halves

1. Preheat oven to 350°F. Squeeze 3 tablespoons juice from lemons; reserve squeezed lemon halves. Combine lemon juice, parsley, mustard, garlic, oil, rosemary, pepper and salt in small bowl; mix well. Reserve 2 tablespoons mixture.

2. Place chicken on rack in roasting or baking pan. Gently slide fingers between skin and meat of chicken breasts and drumsticks to separate skin from meat, being careful not to tear skin. Spoon parsley mixture under loosened skin. (Secure breast skin with toothpicks, if necessary.) Discard any remaining parsley mixture. Place lemon halves in cavity of chicken. Roast 30 minutes.

3. Meanwhile, toss potatoes with reserved parsley mixture in medium bowl until coated. Arrange potatoes around chicken; roast 1 hour or until meat thermometer inserted into thickest part of thigh registers 165°F.

4. Transfer chicken to cutting board. Tent with foil; let stand 10 minutes. Remove skin; slice chicken. Sprinkle any accumulated parsley mixture from pan over chicken and potatoes. *Makes 6 servings*

Nutrients per Serving:
Calories: 294, **Calories from Fat:** 27%, **Total Fat:** 9g, **Saturated Fat:** 2g, **Cholesterol:** 84mg, **Sodium:** 348mg, **Carbohydrate:** 26g, **Fiber:** 3g, **Protein:** 30g

Dietary Exchanges: 2 Starch, 3 Meat

Lemon-Dijon Chicken
with Potatoes

Poached Salmon with Dill-Lemon Sauce

Poaching Liquid
>   3 cups water
>   1 cup white wine
>   Peel of 1 lemon
>   3 black peppercorns
>   4 sprigs fresh parsley
>   2 sprigs fresh dill
>   1 shallot, cut crosswise into thin slices
>   2 salmon fillets (6 ounces each), about 1 inch thick

Dill-Lemon Sauce
>   1½ teaspoons lemon juice
>   1 teaspoon canola oil
>   2 tablespoons low-fat mayonnaise
>   2 tablespoons milk
>   1 teaspoon chopped fresh dill
>   Additional fresh dill sprigs (optional)

1. Combine water, wine, lemon peel, peppercorns, parsley, dill sprigs and shallot in medium saucepan. Bring to a simmer; do not boil. Simmer 15 minutes.

2. Reduce heat to just below simmering. Place salmon in liquid; cook 4 to 5 minutes or until fish begins to flake when tested with fork.

3. Meanwhile, prepare sauce. Whisk lemon juice and oil in small bowl. Add mayonnaise; mix well. (Mixture may look separated, but will come together after beating.) Stir in milk, 1 teaspoon at a time, mixing well after each addition. Stir in chopped dill just before serving.

4. Transfer salmon to serving plates. Top with sauce; garnish with dill sprigs. *Makes 2 servings*

Nutrients per Serving: 1 salmon fillet with about 2½ tablespoons sauce
Calories: 387, **Calories from Fat:** 55%, **Total Fat:** 23g, **Saturated Fat:** 6g,
Cholesterol: 89mg, **Sodium:** 169mg, **Carbohydrate:** 4g, **Fiber:** 0g, **Protein:** 35g

Dietary Exchanges: 5 Meat, 2½ Fat

*Poached Salmon with
Dill-Lemon Sauce*

Classic Turkey Pot Pie

Filling
  2 teaspoons olive oil
  1 cup diced red bell pepper
  2 stalks celery, sliced
  1 small onion, chopped
  2 tablespoons all-purpose flour
1¼ cups fat-free reduced-sodium chicken broth
  1 cup cubed peeled potato
  ½ teaspoon dried thyme
  ¼ teaspoon salt
  ¼ teaspoon black pepper
  2 cups cubed cooked turkey breast (about 10 ounces)
  ⅓ cup frozen peas

Biscuit Topping
  ¾ cup all-purpose flour
  ¾ teaspoon baking powder
  ⅛ teaspoon salt
  ⅛ teaspoon baking soda
  3 tablespoons cold reduced-fat stick margarine, cubed
  3 to 5 tablespoons buttermilk

1. Preheat oven to 425°F.

2. For filling, heat oil in large skillet over medium heat. Add bell pepper, celery and onion; cook and stir 4 to 5 minutes. Stir in flour until blended. Stir in broth, potato, thyme, salt and black pepper; bring to a boil. Reduce heat; cover and simmer 8 to 10 minutes.

3. Stir in turkey and peas; simmer 5 to 7 minutes or until potato is tender and peas are hot. Pour into 1- to 1½-quart casserole.

continued on page 76

Classic Turkey Pot Pie

Classic Turkey Pot Pie, continued

4. For topping, combine flour, baking powder, salt and baking soda in medium bowl. Cut in margarine with pastry blender or 2 knives until margarine is size of peas. Stir in buttermilk until dough forms.

5. Place dough on floured surface; knead lightly. Pat out to about ½-inch thickness. Cut into 5 biscuits with 2- to 2½-inch biscuit cutter, rerolling dough as needed. Place biscuits on top of filling.

6. Bake 12 to 14 minutes or until lightly browned.   *Makes 5 servings*

Note: This fast and delicious recipe will please both adults and children. The recipe is quicker than it looks, because most of the ingredients are common pantry staples. The fresh (and frozen) vegetables make it a healthy version of an old favorite. You can substitute the vegetables in the recipe for other vegetables you may have on hand, such as broccoli, carrots or cauliflower.

Nutrients per Serving: 1 biscuit and ¾ cup turkey mixture
Calories: 250, **Calories from Fat:** 18%, **Total Fat:** 5g, **Saturated Fat:** 1g, **Cholesterol:** 38mg, **Sodium:** 505mg, **Carbohydrate:** 30g, **Fiber:** 3g, **Protein:** 18g

Dietary Exchanges: 2 Starch, 2 Meat, 1 Fat

For the most tender biscuits, make sure the margarine is very cold, and don't overwork the dough—too much handling and re-rolling will result in tough biscuits.

Lamb Chops with Cranberry-Pear Chutney

½ cup water
¼ cup dried cranberries
¼ cup dried apricots, cut into quarters
¼ cup no-sugar-added raspberry fruit spread
1 tablespoon red wine vinegar
¼ teaspoon ground cinnamon
¼ teaspoon plus ⅛ teaspoon salt, divided
1 medium pear, peeled and cut into ½-inch pieces
½ teaspoon vanilla
4 bone-in lamb loin chops (about 5 ounces each)
2 cloves garlic, minced
¼ teaspoon dried rosemary
   Black pepper

1. Preheat broiler. Spray broiler pan and rack with nonstick cooking spray.

2. For chutney, combine water, cranberries, apricots, fruit spread, vinegar, cinnamon and ⅛ teaspoon salt in medium saucepan; bring to a boil over high heat. Reduce heat to medium-low; simmer, uncovered, 12 minutes or until mixture is thickened. Remove from heat; stir in pear and vanilla.

3. Rub both sides of lamb chops with garlic. Sprinkle with rosemary, remaining ¼ teaspoon salt and pepper to taste; arrange lamb chops on prepared rack.

4. Broil lamb at least 5 inches from heat source 7 minutes. Turn and broil 7 minutes more or until desired doneness. Serve lamb chops with chutney.   *Makes 4 servings*

Nutrients per Serving: 1 lamb chop with ¼ cup chutney
Calories: 260, **Calories from Fat:** 28%, **Total Fat:** 8g, **Saturated Fat:** 3g,
Cholesterol: 71mg, **Sodium:** 293mg, **Carbohydrate:** 24g, **Fiber:** 2g, **Protein:** 22g

Dietary Exchanges: 1½ Fruit, 3 Meat

Seared Spiced Pork Tenderloin and Apples

½ teaspoon ground cinnamon
½ teaspoon ground cumin
½ teaspoon black pepper
¼ teaspoon salt
⅛ teaspoon ground allspice
1 pound pork tenderloin
1 teaspoon canola oil
2 medium Fuji or Gala apples, sliced
¼ cup raisins
¼ cup water
2 teaspoons diet margarine

1. Preheat oven to 425°F. Line baking sheet with foil. Combine cinnamon, cumin, pepper, salt and allspice in small bowl; mix well. Sprinkle evenly over all sides of pork, pressing to adhere.

2. Heat oil in large skillet over medium-high heat. Add pork; cook until browned on all sides, turning frequently. Place pork on prepared baking sheet; reserve skillet for cooking apples.

3. Roast 18 minutes or until meat thermometer inserted into center of tenderloin registers 155°F. Transfer pork to cutting board; let stand 5 minutes before cutting into thin slices.

4. Meanwhile, place apples, raisins and water in skillet; cook and stir over medium-high heat 1 to 2 minutes or until apples begin to brown. Remove from heat; stir in margarine. Cover and let stand until ready to serve. To serve, place about ⅓ cup apple mixture on each of 4 plates; top with pork slices. *Makes 4 servings*

Nutrients per Serving: 3 ounces pork with ⅓ cup apple mixture
Calories: 217, **Calories from Fat:** 22%, **Total Fat:** 6g, **Saturated Fat:** 2g, **Cholesterol:** 73mg, **Sodium:** 216mg, **Carbohydrate:** 17g, **Fiber:** 2g, **Protein:** 26g

Dietary Exchanges: 1 Fruit, 3 Meat

*Seared Spiced Pork Tenderloin
and Apples*

Thyme-Scented Roasted Sweet Potatoes and Onions

2 large sweet potatoes (about 1¼ pounds), unpeeled and scrubbed
1 medium sweet or yellow onion, cut into chunks
2 tablespoons canola oil
1 teaspoon dried thyme
½ teaspoon salt
½ teaspoon smoked paprika
⅛ teaspoon ground red pepper (optional)

1. Preheat oven to 425°F. Spray 15×10-inch jelly-roll pan with nonstick cooking spray.

2. Cut sweet potatoes into 1-inch chunks; place in large bowl. Add onion, oil, thyme, salt, paprika and red pepper, if desired; toss to coat. Spread vegetables in single layer on prepared pan.

3. Roast 25 to 30 minutes or until very tender, stirring after 10 minutes. Let stand 5 minutes before serving. *Makes 10 servings*

Nutrients per Serving: ½ cup
Calories: 78, **Calories from Fat:** 32%, **Total Fat:** 3g, **Saturated Fat:** <1g,
Cholesterol: 0mg, **Sodium:** 148mg, **Carbohydrate:** 13g, **Fiber:** 2g, **Protein:** 1g

Dietary Exchanges: 1 Starch, ½ Fat

Thyme-Scented Roasted
Sweet Potatoes and Onions

Mediterranean Orzo and Vegetable Pilaf

½ cup plus 2 tablespoons (4 ounces) uncooked orzo pasta
2 teaspoons olive oil
1 small onion, diced
2 cloves garlic, minced
1 small zucchini, diced
½ cup fat-free reduced-sodium chicken broth
1 can (about 14 ounces) artichoke hearts, drained and quartered
1 medium tomato, chopped
½ teaspoon dried oregano
½ teaspoon salt
¼ teaspoon black pepper
½ cup crumbled feta cheese
  Sliced black olives (optional)

1. Cook orzo according to package directions, omitting salt. Drain; keep warm.

2. Heat oil in large nonstick skillet over medium heat. Add onion; cook and stir 5 minutes or until tender. Add garlic; cook and stir 1 minute.

3. Stir in zucchini and broth. Reduce heat; simmer about 5 minutes or until zucchini is crisp-tender.

4. Add orzo, artichokes, tomato, oregano, salt and pepper to skillet; cook and stir about 1 minute or until heated through. Sprinkle with feta. Top with olives, if desired.   *Makes 6 servings*

Nutrients per Serving: ½ cup
Calories: 168, **Calories from Fat:** 33%, **Total Fat:** 7g, **Saturated Fat:** 2g, **Cholesterol:** 11mg, **Sodium:** 516mg, **Carbohydrate:** 23g, **Fiber:** 3g, **Protein:** 7g

Dietary Exchanges: 1½ Vegetable, 1 Starch, ½ Meat, 1 Fat

*Mediterranean Orzo and
Vegetable Pilaf*

Peppery Green Beans

  2 tablespoons olive oil
  2 teaspoons Worcestershire sauce
½ teaspoon garlic salt
½ teaspoon black pepper
  1 pound whole green beans, stemmed, rinsed and patted dry
  1 medium onion, cut into ½-inch wedges
  1 medium red bell pepper, cut into ½-inch slices
     Salt (optional)

1. Preheat oven to 450°F. Line baking sheet with foil. Combine oil, Worcestershire sauce, garlic salt and black pepper in small bowl; mix well.

2. Place beans, onion and bell pepper on prepared baking sheet. Pour half of oil mixture over vegetables; toss to coat. Spread vegetables in single layer.

3. Roast 20 to 25 minutes or until vegetables begin to brown, stirring every 5 minutes. Add remaining oil mixture and salt to taste, if desired; toss to coat. *Makes 8 servings*

Nutrients per Serving: ½ cup
Calories: 58, **Calories from Fat:** 52%, **Total Fat:** 3g, **Saturated Fat:** <1g, **Cholesterol:** 0mg, **Sodium:** 82mg, **Carbohydrate:** 5g, **Fiber:** 2g, **Protein:** 1g

Dietary Exchanges: 1 Vegetable, ½ Fat

Peppery Green Beans

Savory Bread Stuffing

  2 teaspoons canola oil
½ cup chopped onion
½ cup chopped celery
  1 cup fat-free reduced-sodium chicken broth
½ cup unsweetened apple juice
  4 cups (7 ounces) seasoned cubed bread stuffing mix
¾ cup diced unpeeled red apple
¼ cup chopped pecans, toasted*

*To toast pecans, spread in single layer on ungreased baking sheet. Bake in preheated 350°F oven 5 to 7 minutes or until fragrant, stirring occasionally.

1. Preheat oven to 350°F. Spray 2- to 2½-quart casserole with nonstick cooking spray.

2. Heat oil in medium saucepan over medium heat. Add onion and celery; cook and stir 7 to 8 minutes or until vegetables are tender and lightly browned on edges.

3. Stir in broth and juice; bring to a boil over high heat. Remove from heat; stir in stuffing mix, apple and pecans. Transfer to prepared casserole.

4. Cover and bake 30 to 35 minutes or until heated through.

Makes 12 servings

Variations: If your diet plan permits, stir in 2 tablespoons light butter with canola oil at the end of the cooking time. Sprinkle with additional pecans.

Nutrients per Serving: ½ cup
Calories: 111, **Calories from Fat:** 25%, **Total Fat:** 3g, **Saturated Fat:** <1g, **Cholesterol:** 0mg, **Sodium:** 317mg, **Carbohydrate:** 18g, **Fiber:** 2g, **Protein:** 3g

Dietary Exchanges: 1 Starch, 1 Fat

Savory Bread Stuffing

Asparagus with No-Cook Creamy Mustard Sauce

½ cup plain fat-free yogurt
2 tablespoons reduced-fat mayonnaise
1 tablespoon Dijon mustard
2 teaspoons lemon juice
½ teaspoon salt
2 cups water
1½ pounds asparagus spears, trimmed
⅛ teaspoon black pepper (optional)

1. Whisk yogurt, mayonnaise, mustard, lemon juice and salt in small bowl until smooth; set aside.

2. Bring water to a boil in large skillet over high heat. Add asparagus; return to a boil. Reduce heat; cover and simmer 3 minutes or until crisp-tender. Drain well.

3. Place asparagus on serving platter; top with sauce. Sprinkle with pepper, if desired. *Makes 6 servings*

Nutrients per Serving: about 6 asparagus spears with 2 tablespoons sauce
Calories: 57, **Calories from Fat:** 28%, **Total Fat:** 2g, **Saturated Fat:** <1g,
Cholesterol: 2mg, **Sodium:** 299mg, **Carbohydrate:** 8g, **Fiber:** 2g, **Protein:** 4g

Dietary Exchanges: 2 Vegetable

*Asparagus with No-Cook
Creamy Mustard Sauce*

Potato-Cauliflower Mash

  3 cups water
  2 cups cubed unpeeled Yukon Gold potatoes (about 12 ounces)
  10 ounces frozen cauliflower florets
  ¼ cup fat-free evaporated milk
  2 tablespoons trans-fat-free margarine
  ¾ teaspoon salt
  ¼ teaspoon black pepper

1. Bring water to a boil in large saucepan. Add potatoes and cauliflower; return to a boil. Reduce heat; cover and simmer 10 minutes or until potatoes are tender.

2. Drain vegetables; place in blender with evaporated milk, margarine, salt and pepper. Blend until smooth, scraping side frequently.

Makes 4 servings

Nutrients per Serving: ½ cup
Calories: 173, Calories from Fat: 32%, Total Fat: 6g, Saturated Fat: 1g, Cholesterol: 0mg, Sodium: 531mg, Carbohydrate: 25g, Fiber: 3g, Protein: 4g

Dietary Exchanges: 2 Vegetable, 1 Starch, 1 Fat

Chutney Glazed Carrots

  2 cups cut peeled carrots (1½-inch pieces)
  3 tablespoons cranberry or mango chutney
  1 tablespoon Dijon mustard
  2 teaspoons butter
  2 tablespoons chopped pecans, toasted*

*To toast pecans, place in small skillet; cook over medium heat 5 minutes or until fragrant, stirring occasionally.

1. Place carrots in medium saucepan; cover with water. Bring to a boil over high heat. Reduce heat; simmer 6 to 8 minutes or until carrots are tender.

2. Drain carrots; return to pan. Add chutney, mustard and butter; cook and stir over medium heat about 2 minutes or until carrots are glazed. Sprinkle with pecans. *Makes 4 servings*

Nutrients per Serving: ½ cup
Calories: 88, **Calories from Fat:** 48%, **Total Fat:** 5g, **Saturated Fat:** 1g, **Cholesterol:** 5mg, **Sodium:** 151mg, **Carbohydrate:** 11g, **Fiber:** 2g, **Protein:** 1g

Dietary Exchanges: ½ Starch, 1 Fat

Vegetable Medley Rice Pilaf

    1 cup fresh broccoli florets
    1 large carrot, shredded
    1 small red onion or 1 large shallot, chopped
    1 cup uncooked instant brown rice
    1 teaspoon olive oil
    ¼ teaspoon dried thyme
    1 cup fat-free reduced-sodium chicken or vegetable broth
    ⅛ teaspoon black pepper

1. Spray large nonstick skillet with nonstick cooking spray. Add broccoli, carrot and onion; cook and stir over medium heat 5 to 8 minutes or until crisp-tender. Add rice, oil and thyme; cook 1 minute, stirring constantly to coat rice with oil.

2. Stir in broth; bring to a boil. Reduce heat to low; cover and simmer 5 minutes. Remove from heat; let stand 5 minutes.

3. Fluff pilaf with fork and season with pepper before serving.
Makes 4 servings

Nutrients per Serving: ½ cup
Calories: 210, **Calories from Fat:** 10%, **Total Fat:** 2g, **Saturated Fat:** <1g, **Cholesterol:** 0mg, **Sodium:** 178mg, **Carbohydrate:** 42g, **Fiber:** 3g, **Protein:** 6g

Dietary Exchanges: 3 Starch

Cranberry-Apple Chutney

1 cup sweet onion, chopped
1 cup sucralose-based sugar substitute
¾ cup unsweetened apple juice
½ cup packed light brown sugar
1 teaspoon ground cinnamon
½ teaspoon ground ginger
⅛ teaspoon ground cloves
1 package (12 ounces) fresh or frozen cranberries
1 large Granny Smith apple, peeled and cut into ½-inch pieces

1. Combine onion, sugar substitute, juice, brown sugar, cinnamon, ginger and cloves in medium heavy saucepan; bring to a boil over high heat. Reduce heat and simmer, uncovered, 5 minutes.

2. Stir in cranberries and apple; simmer, uncovered, 20 minutes or until mixture is very thick, stirring occasionally.

3. Cool to room temperature. Transfer to serving dish or refrigerate until ready to serve. *Makes 20 servings*

Nutrients per Serving: 2 tablespoons
Calories: 41, **Calories from Fat:** 1%, **Total Fat:** <1g, **Saturated Fat:** <1g, **Cholesterol:** 0mg, **Sodium:** 3mg, **Carbohydrate:** 12g, **Fiber:** 1g, **Protein:** <1g

Dietary Exchanges: 1 Fruit

Cranberry-Apple Chutney

Festive Corn Casserole

2 cups grated zucchini
1 cup frozen corn
1 cup diced red bell pepper
2 cups cholesterol-free egg substitute
½ cup evaporated fat-free milk
2 teaspoons sugar substitute
¼ teaspoon celery seed
⅛ teaspoon salt
⅛ teaspoon red pepper flakes (optional)

1. Preheat oven to 350°F. Spray 11×7-inch baking dish with nonstick cooking spray.

2. Combine zucchini, corn and bell pepper in prepared dish. Whisk egg substitute, evaporated milk, sugar substitute, celery seed, salt and red pepper flakes, if desired, in large bowl. Pour egg mixture over vegetables in baking dish.

3. Bake 45 to 55 minutes or until top of casserole is golden brown.

Makes 10 servings

Nutrients per Serving: about ½ cup
Calories: 54, **Calories from Fat:** <1%, **Total Fat:** <1g, **Saturated Fat:** 0g, **Cholesterol:** <1mg, **Sodium:** 138mg, **Carbohydrate:** 7g, **Fiber:** 1g, **Protein:** 6g

Dietary Exchanges: 1 Vegetable, 1 Meat

Festive Corn Casserole

Parmesan-Pepper Cloverleaf Rolls

¾ cup plus 2 tablespoons grated Parmesan cheese, divided
½ teaspoon black pepper
1 loaf (1 pound) frozen bread dough, thawed

1. Knead ¾ cup cheese and pepper into bread dough, adding cheese 2 to 3 tablespoons at a time, until evenly mixed. Divide dough into 12 equal pieces; shape into balls. Cover with plastic wrap; let rest 10 minutes.

2. Spray 12 standard (2½-inch) muffin cups and hands with nonstick cooking spray. Divide each ball of dough into 3 pieces; roll each piece into small ball. Place 3 balls in each muffin cup. Cover rolls loosely with plastic wrap; let rise in warm place about 30 minutes or until doubled.

3. Preheat oven to 350°F. Sprinkle rolls with remaining 2 tablespoons cheese. Bake 12 to 15 minutes or until golden brown.

Makes 12 servings

Nutrients per Serving: 1 roll
Calories: 140, **Calories from Fat:** 27%, **Total Fat:** 4g, **Saturated Fat:** 2g,
Cholesterol: 9mg, **Sodium:** 307mg, **Carbohydrate:** 20g, **Fiber:** 1g, **Protein:** 7g

Dietary Exchanges: 1½ Starch, ½ Meat

Parmesan-Pepper Cloverleaf Rolls

Winter Squash Risotto

2 tablespoons olive oil

2 cups butternut or delicata squash (1 small butternut squash or
  1 medium delicata), peeled and cut into 1-inch pieces

1 large shallot or 1 small onion, finely chopped

½ teaspoon paprika

¼ teaspoon salt

¼ teaspoon dried thyme

¼ teaspoon black pepper

1 cup uncooked arborio rice

¼ cup dry white wine (optional)

4 to 5 cups hot reduced-sodium vegetable or chicken broth

½ cup grated Parmesan or Romano cheese

1. Heat oil in large saucepan over medium heat. Add squash; cook and stir 3 minutes. Add shallot; cook and stir 3 to 4 minutes or until squash is almost tender. Stir in paprika, salt, thyme and pepper. Add rice; stir to coat with oil.

2. Add wine, if desired; cook and stir until wine evaporates. Add ½ cup broth; cook, stirring occasionally, until rice is almost dry. Stir in another ½ cup broth; continue to cook and stir rice occasionally, adding ½ cup broth each time previous addition is absorbed. Rice is done when consistency is creamy and grains are tender with slight resistance. (Total cooking time will be 20 to 30 minutes.)

3. Stir in Parmesan. Serve immediately.   *Makes 6 servings*

Nutrients per Serving:
Calories: 230, **Calories from Fat:** 32%, **Total Fat:** 8g, **Saturated Fat:** 3g, **Cholesterol:** 10mg, **Sodium:** 640mg, **Carbohydrate:** 32g, **Fiber:** 2g, **Protein:** 10g

Dietary Exchanges: 2 Starch, 1 Fat, ½ Meat

Winter Squash Risotto

Glazed Parsnips and Carrots

1 pound parsnips (2 large or 3 medium)
1 package (8 ounces) baby carrots
1 tablespoon canola oil
Salt and black pepper (optional)
¼ cup orange juice
1 tablespoon butter
1 tablespoon honey
⅛ teaspoon ground ginger

1. Preheat oven to 425°F. Peel parsnips; cut into wedges to match size of baby carrots.

2. Spread vegetables in shallow roasting pan. Drizzle with oil and season with salt and pepper, if desired; toss to coat. Roast 30 to 35 minutes or until vegetables are fork-tender.

3. Combine orange juice, butter, honey and ginger in large skillet. Add vegetables; cook and stir over high heat 1 to 2 minutes or until sauce thickens and coats vegetables. *Makes 6 servings*

Nutrients per Serving:
Calories: 123, **Calories from Fat:** 33%, **Total Fat:** 5g, **Saturated Fat:** 1g, **Cholesterol:** 5mg, **Sodium:** 38mg, **Carbohydrate:** 20g, **Fiber:** 4g, **Protein:** 1g

Dietary Exchanges: 1 Starch

Glazed Parsnips and Carrots

Brussels Sprouts with Walnuts

1 cup diced butternut squash (1-inch cubes)
1 pound brussels sprouts, trimmed
2 cups water
1 cup apple juice
½ cup fat-free vinaigrette salad dressing
1 cup arugula, mixed baby lettuce or baby spinach leaves
½ cup chopped walnuts, toasted*

To toast walnuts, spread in single layer on baking sheet. Bake in preheated 350°F oven 5 to 7 minutes or until fragrant, stirring occasionally.

1. Preheat oven to 400°F. Lightly spray baking sheet with nonstick cooking spray. Place squash in single layer on prepared baking sheet; roast 20 minutes or until tender. Cool 5 minutes.

2. Meanwhile, combine brussels sprouts, water and apple juice in medium saucepan. Simmer over medium heat 15 minutes or until sprouts are tender. Rinse under cold water; drain well.

3. When cool enough to handle, cut sprouts lengthwise into thin slices. Combine with warm squash; toss with salad dressing until coated.

4. Divide greens among 4 serving plates. Spoon vegetables over greens; sprinkle with walnuts.   *Makes 4 servings*

Nutrients per Serving: 1 cup
Calories: 190, **Calories from Fat:** 39%, **Total Fat:** 10g, **Saturated Fat:** 1g, **Cholesterol:** 0mg, **Sodium:** 204mg, **Carbohydrate:** 20g, **Fiber:** 6g, **Protein:** 7g

Dietary Exchanges: 1 Starch, 1 Vegetable, 2 Fat

Brussels Sprouts with Walnuts

Corn Bread, Bacon & Sage Dressing

1 package (6½ ounces) corn bread mix
⅓ cup fat-free (skim) milk
2 egg whites
2 tablespoons plus 1 teaspoon canola oil, divided
1 cup diced onion (1 medium onion)
¾ cup diced celery (2 stalks)
2 tablespoons bacon bits
1 teaspoon ground sage
½ teaspoon sweet paprika
¼ teaspoon salt
¼ teaspoon black pepper
1¼ cups fat-free reduced-sodium chicken broth

1. Preheat oven to 400°F. Lightly spray 8-inch square baking pan with nonstick cooking spray.

2. Combine corn bread mix, milk, egg whites and 2 tablespoons oil in medium bowl, stirring just until moistened. (Mixture will be lumpy.) Pour batter into prepared pan.

3. Bake 15 to 16 minutes or until firm and brown on edges. Cool in pan on wire rack. Crumble cooled corn bread onto baking sheet. Let stand 1 to 2 hours or until slightly dry.

4. Preheat oven to 350°F. Spray medium baking dish with cooking spray. Heat remaining 1 teaspoon oil in large deep skillet over medium heat. Add onion and celery; cook and stir 3 to 4 minutes or until onion is translucent and celery is crisp-tender. Stir in bacon bits, sage, paprika, salt and pepper. Remove skillet from heat; gently fold in corn bread. Slowly add broth, fluffing lightly with fork. Spoon dressing into prepared dish.

5. Bake about 20 minutes or until lightly browned.   *Makes 8 servings*

Nutrients per Serving: ½ cup
Calories: 160, **Calories from Fat:** 41%, **Total Fat:** 7g, **Saturated Fat:** 1g, **Cholesterol:** 3mg, **Sodium:** 432mg, **Carbohydrate:** 19g, **Fiber:** 2g, **Protein:** 5g

Dietary Exchanges: 1 Starch, 1½ Fat

Glazed Maple Acorn Squash

1 large acorn squash
¼ cup water
2 tablespoons pure maple syrup
1 tablespoon margarine or butter, melted
¼ teaspoon ground cinnamon

1. Preheat oven to 375°F. Cut stem and blossom ends from squash. Cut squash crosswise into 4 or 5 equal slices; discard seeds and membrane.

2. Place water in 13×9-inch baking dish. Arrange squash in dish; cover with foil. Bake 30 minutes or until tender.

3. Combine maple syrup, margarine and cinnamon in small bowl; mix well. Uncover squash; pour off water. Brush squash with syrup mixture, letting excess pool in center of squash rings.

4. Bake 10 minutes or until syrup mixture is bubbly.

Makes 4 to 5 servings

Nutrients per Serving:
Calories: 90, **Calories from Fat:** 30%, **Total Fat:** 3g, **Saturated Fat:** 1g, **Cholesterol:** 8mg, **Sodium:** 39mg, **Carbohydrate:** 18g, **Fiber:** 2g, **Protein:** 1g

Dietary Exchanges: 1 Starch, ½ Fat

Choose a squash that is heavy for its size with a hard shell that is free of blemishes. Acorn squash can be stored in a cool dark place for several months.

Quinoa with Roasted Vegetables

2 medium sweet potatoes, cut into ½-inch-thick slices
1 medium eggplant, peeled and cut into ½-inch cubes
1 medium tomato, cut into wedges
1 large green bell pepper, sliced
1 small onion, cut into wedges
½ teaspoon salt
¼ teaspoon black pepper
¼ teaspoon ground red pepper
1 cup uncooked quinoa
2 cloves garlic, minced
½ teaspoon dried thyme
¼ teaspoon dried marjoram
2 cups water or fat-free reduced-sodium chicken broth

1. Preheat oven to 450°F. Line large jelly-roll pan with foil; spray with nonstick cooking spray.

2. Place sweet potatoes, eggplant, tomato, bell pepper and onion on prepared pan; spray lightly with cooking spray. Sprinkle with salt, black pepper and ground red pepper; toss to coat. Roast 20 to 30 minutes or until vegetables are tender and browned.

3. Meanwhile, place quinoa in strainer; rinse well. Spray medium saucepan with cooking spray; heat over medium heat. Add garlic, thyme and marjoram; cook and stir 1 to 2 minutes. Add quinoa; cook and stir 2 to 3 minutes. Stir in water; bring to a boil over high heat. Reduce heat to low; cover and simmer 15 to 20 minutes or until water is absorbed. (Quinoa will appear somewhat translucent.) Transfer quinoa to large bowl; gently stir in vegetables.

Makes 6 servings

Nutrients per Serving:
Calories: 193, **Calories from Fat:** 9%, **Total Fat:** 2g, **Saturated Fat:** <1g,
Cholesterol: 0mg, **Sodium:** 194mg, **Carbohydrate:** 40g, **Fiber:** 6g, **Protein:** 6g

Dietary Exchanges: ½ Vegetable, 2½ Starch

Quinoa with Roasted Vegetables

Chocolate Peanut Butter Truffles

½ cup reduced-fat chunky peanut butter
3 tablespoons sugar substitute*
1 cup crisp rice cereal
3 tablespoons unsweetened cocoa powder
¼ cup semisweet chocolate chips

This recipe was tested using sucralose-based sugar substitute.

1. Place peanut butter in small microwavable bowl. Microwave on HIGH 10 seconds. Stir in sugar substitute until smooth. Stir in cereal; mix well.

2. Line large plate with waxed paper. Spray hands with nonstick cooking spray. Shape peanut butter mixture into 1-inch balls, pressing firmly. Place balls on prepared plate; freeze 15 minutes or up to 1 hour.

3. Place cocoa in shallow dish. Roll each truffle in cocoa; return to plate.

4. Place chocolate chips in small resealable food storage bag. Microwave on HIGH 10 seconds; knead bag. Repeat until chocolate is melted and smooth.

5. Press melted chocolate into one corner of bag; cut very small hole in corner. Drizzle chocolate over truffles. Let chocolate set before serving. Truffles can be refrigerated in airtight container up to 3 days.

Makes 20 truffles

Nutrients per Serving: 4 truffles
Calories: 220, **Calories from Fat:** 49%, **Total Fat:** 12g, **Saturated Fat:** 3g, **Cholesterol:** 0mg, **Sodium:** 229mg, **Carbohydrate:** 25g, **Fiber:** 3g, **Protein:** 8g

Dietary Exchanges: ½ Starch, 2 Fat

Chocolate Peanut Butter Truffles

Orange Almond Cake

⅔ cup all-purpose flour, plus additional for dusting pan
1 teaspoon baking powder
¼ teaspoon baking soda
¼ teaspoon salt
¾ cup granulated sugar
¼ cup almond paste
2 eggs
½ cup cholesterol-free egg substitute
2 teaspoons grated orange peel
1 teaspoon vanilla
2 teaspoons powdered sugar
    Fresh berries (optional)

1. Preheat oven to 350°F. Cut circle of waxed paper or parchment paper to fit inside 9-inch round springform or cake pan. Spray pan with nonstick cooking spray. Place waxed paper circle on bottom of pan; spray paper with cooking spray and dust with flour.

2. Combine ⅔ cup flour, baking powder, baking soda and salt in small bowl. Beat granulated sugar and almond paste in large bowl with electric mixer at medium speed until blended. Beat in eggs, egg substitute, orange peel and vanilla until well blended. Beat in flour mixture. Pour batter into prepared pan.

3. Bake 35 minutes or until toothpick inserted into center comes out with moist crumbs. Cool completely in pan on wire rack.

4. Remove side of pan; transfer cake to platter. Sprinkle with powdered sugar; serve with berries, if desired.   ***Makes 10 servings***

Nutrients per Serving:
Calories: 139, **Calories from Fat:** 19%, **Total Fat:** 3g, **Saturated Fat:** <1g, **Cholesterol:** 42mg, **Sodium:** 176mg, **Carbohydrate:** 25g, **Fiber:** 1g, **Protein:** 4g

Dietary Exchanges: 1½ Starch, ½ Fat

Orange Almond Cake

Crème Caramel

½ cup sugar, divided
1 tablespoon hot water
2 cups fat-free (skim) milk
⅛ teaspoon salt
½ cup cholesterol-free egg substitute
½ teaspoon vanilla
⅛ teaspoon maple extract

1. Heat ¼ cup sugar in heavy saucepan over low heat, stirring constantly until melted and straw colored. Remove from heat; stir in water. Return to heat; cook and stir 5 minutes or until mixture is dark caramel color. Divide melted sugar evenly among 6 (4-ounce) custard cups.

2. Preheat oven to 350°F. Combine milk, remaining ¼ cup sugar and salt in medium bowl. Add egg substitute, vanilla and maple extract; mix well. Pour ½ cup mixture into each custard cup. Place cups in heavy baking or roasting pan; pour 1 to 2 inches hot water into pan to reach halfway up sides of cups.

3. Bake 40 to 45 minutes or until knife inserted near edge of each cup comes out clean. Remove cups from baking pan; cool on wire rack.

4. Refrigerate 4 hours or overnight. Before serving, run knife around edge of each cup. Invert custard onto serving plate; remove cup.

Makes 6 servings

Nutrients per Serving: 1 custard
Calories: 104, **Calories from Fat:** 1%, **Total Fat:** <1g, **Saturated Fat:** 0g, **Cholesterol:** 2mg, **Sodium:** 121mg, **Carbohydrate:** 21g, **Fiber:** 0g, **Protein:** 5g

Dietary Exchanges: 1½ Starch, ½ Milk

Crème Caramel

Apple Galette

¾ cup all-purpose flour
¼ cup whole wheat flour
 1 teaspoon baking powder
⅛ teaspoon salt
¼ cup (½ stick) cold margarine
 3 tablespoons plus 1 teaspoon cold fat-free (skim) milk, divided
 3 cups thinly sliced peeled baking apples
 2 tablespoons sugar
 1 teaspoon ground cinnamon

1. Preheat oven to 375°F. Combine all-purpose flour, whole wheat flour, baking powder and salt in medium bowl. Cut in margarine until mixture resembles coarse crumbs. Add 3 tablespoons milk, 1 tablespoon at a time, mixing with fork until dough is moistened. (Dough will be crumbly.)

2. Turn dough out onto lightly floured surface; knead 6 to 8 times or just until dough clings together. Form into a ball. Roll dough into 12-inch circle on parchment paper or heavy-duty foil. Transfer to large baking sheet.

3. Combine apples, sugar and cinnamon in medium bowl; toss to coat. Mound apple mixture in center of dough, leaving 2-inch border. Fold border up over filling. Brush top and side of crust with remaining 1 teaspoon milk. Cover edge of crust with foil.

4. Bake 15 minutes; remove foil. Bake about 25 minutes or until crust is golden and apples are tender. Cool 10 minutes on baking sheet. Transfer to wire rack; cool 20 minutes. Serve warm.   *Makes 6 servings*

Nutrients per Serving:
Calories: 190, **Calories from Fat:** 38%, **Total Fat:** 8g, **Saturated Fat:** 2g, **Cholesterol:** 0mg, **Sodium:** 210mg, **Carbohydrate:** 28g, **Fiber:** 2g, **Protein:** 3g

Dietary Exchanges: 1 Fruit, 1 Starch

Apple Galette

Italian Cheesecake

9 graham crackers
⅓ cup packed brown sugar
3 tablespoons butter, melted
2 packages (8 ounces each) fat-free cream cheese, softened
1½ cups sugar substitute*
1 container (15 ounces) fat-free ricotta cheese
2 eggs
½ cup cholesterol-free egg substitute
3 tablespoons cornstarch
3 tablespoons all-purpose flour
1 teaspoon vanilla
2 cups reduced-fat sour cream
Fresh strawberries and mint leaves (optional)

This recipe was tested using sucralose-based sugar substitute.

1. Spray 9-inch springform pan with nonstick cooking spray.

2. Place graham crackers in resealable food storage bag; crush into fine crumbs with rolling pin. Mix crumbs and brown sugar in small bowl; stir in butter until crumbs are moistened. Press crumbs into bottom and 1 inch up side of prepared pan. Refrigerate crust while preparing filling.

3. Preheat oven to 300°F. Beat cream cheese and sugar substitute in large bowl with electric mixer at medium speed until smooth. Add ricotta; beat until blended. Slowly add eggs and egg substitute; beat until well blended. Beat in cornstarch, flour and vanilla. Beat in sour cream just until blended. Pour filling into prepared crust; place pan on baking sheet.

4. Bake 1 hour and 30 minutes to 1 hour and 40 minutes or until top of cheesecake is golden and just set. Cool completely in pan on wire rack. Refrigerate 8 hours or overnight. Garnish with strawberries and mint.

Makes 18 servings

Nutrients per Serving:
Calories: 154, **Calories from Fat:** 41%, **Total Fat:** 7g, **Saturated Fat:** 3g, **Cholesterol:** 47mg, **Sodium:** 296mg, **Carbohydrate:** 15g, **Fiber:** <1g, **Protein:** 10g

Dietary Exchanges: 1 Starch, 1 Meat, ½ Fat

Italian Cheesecake

Poached Pears in Cinnamon-Apricot Sauce

1 can (5½ ounces) apricot nectar
1 tablespoon sugar
1 teaspoon lemon juice
½ teaspoon ground cinnamon
¼ teaspoon grated lemon peel
⅛ teaspoon ground cloves
2 large pears
  Fat-free whipped topping (optional)

1. Combine apricot nectar, sugar, lemon juice, cinnamon, lemon peel and cloves in large skillet; bring to a boil over medium-high heat.

2. Meanwhile, cut pears lengthwise into halves, leaving stem attached to one half. Remove cores. Cut pears lengthwise into thin slices, taking care not to cut through stem end. Add pears to skillet with nectar mixture; return to a boil. Reduce heat to medium-low; cover and simmer 6 to 8 minutes or just until pears are tender. Remove pears from skillet, reserving liquid.

3. Simmer liquid, uncovered, over medium heat 2 to 3 minutes or until mixture thickens slightly, stirring occasionally. Fan out pears on dessert plates; spoon sauce over pears. Serve warm or chilled with whipped topping, if desired.   *Makes 4 servings*

Nutrients per Serving: ½ pear with about ½ cup sauce
Calories: 84, **Calories from Fat:** 4%, **Total Fat:** <1g, **Saturated Fat:** <1g, **Cholesterol:** 0mg, **Sodium:** 1mg, **Carbohydrate:** 22g, **Fiber:** 3g, **Protein:** 1g

Dietary Exchanges: 1½ Fruit

Poached Pears in Cinnamon-Apricot Sauce

Carrot Cake with Cream Cheese Glaze

Cake

    2 cups cake flour
    2 teaspoons ground cinnamon
    1 teaspoon baking powder
    1 teaspoon baking soda
    1 teaspoon salt
    ¾ cup sugar substitute*
    ¾ cup packed brown sugar
    ¼ cup vegetable oil
    1 cup cholesterol-free egg substitute
    ½ cup reduced-fat sour cream
    3 cups grated carrots

Glaze

    ½ cup (4 ounces) fat-free cream cheese, softened
    ¼ cup reduced-fat sour cream
    1 tablespoon fat-free (skim) milk
    1 teaspoon vanilla
    ½ cup powdered sugar

This recipe was tested using sucralose-based sugar substitute.

1. Preheat oven to 350°F. Spray 12-cup (10-inch) bundt pan with nonstick cooking spray. Combine flour, cinnamon, baking powder, baking soda and salt in medium bowl.

2. Beat sugar substitute, brown sugar and oil in large bowl with electric mixer at medium speed until blended. Beat in egg substitute and sour cream. Slowly add flour mixture, beating at low speed just until blended. Stir in carrots. Pour batter into prepared pan.

3. Bake about 50 minutes or until toothpick inserted near center comes out clean. Cool in pan 5 minutes. Invert cake onto wire rack; cool completely.

continued on page 122

*Carrot Cake with
Cream Cheese Glaze*

Carrot Cake with Cream Cheese Glaze, continued

4. For glaze, whisk cream cheese, sour cream, milk and vanilla in small bowl until smooth. Whisk in powdered sugar. If glaze is too thick, add water, 1 tablespoon at a time. Spoon glaze over cake.

Makes 16 servings

Nutrients per Serving:
Calories: 176, **Calories from Fat:** 26%, **Total Fat:** 5g, **Saturated Fat:** 1g, **Cholesterol:** 5mg, **Sodium:** 357mg, **Carbohydrate:** 28g, **Fiber:** 1g, **Protein:** 5g

Dietary Exchanges: 2 Starch, 1 Fat

Mint Chocolate Fudge Squares

8 squares (1 ounce each) semisweet chocolate, coarsely chopped, divided
6 squares (1 ounce each) white chocolate, coarsely chopped
1 container (16 ounces) vanilla frosting, divided
4 to 6 drops peppermint extract, divided
3 drops red or green food coloring
½ teaspoon vegetable oil

1. Set aside 1 square semisweet chocolate for garnish. Lightly spray 8-inch square baking pan with nonstick cooking spray. Press parchment paper or waxed paper over bottom and up sides of pan.

2. Combine white chocolate and half of frosting in medium microwavable bowl. Microwave on HIGH 1½ minutes or until melted and smooth, stirring every 30 seconds. Add 2 to 3 drops peppermint extract and food coloring; mix well. Pour into prepared pan; spread evenly. Refrigerate 15 minutes or until set.

3. Combine semisweet chocolate and remaining frosting in medium microwavable bowl. Microwave on HIGH 1½ to 2 minutes or until melted and smooth, stirring every 30 seconds. Add remaining 2 to 3 drops peppermint extract; mix well. Stir 1 to 2 minutes, allowing mixture to cool. Carefully pour over white chocolate layer; spread evenly. Refrigerate 30 minutes or until set.

4. Lift fudge from pan using parchment paper; carefully invert onto cutting board and remove paper. Place reserved semisweet chocolate and oil in small microwavable bowl. Microwave on HIGH 30 seconds or until melted, stirring every 15 seconds. Drizzle melted chocolate over fudge. Refrigerate 20 to 30 minutes or until firm. Cut into 1-inch squares. Store in airtight container in refrigerator. *Makes 64 squares*

Nutrients per Serving: 2 squares
Calories: 126, **Calories from Fat:** 43%, **Total Fat:** 6g, **Saturated Fat:** 3g, **Cholesterol:** 0mg, **Sodium:** 32mg, **Carbohydrate:** 17g, **Fiber:** 1g, **Protein:** 1g

Dietary Exchanges: 1 Starch, 1 Fat

Sweet Potato-Ginger Cake

    1 package (about 18 ounces) spice cake mix
1⅓ cups water
    1 cup mashed sweet potatoes*
    6 egg whites *or* ¾ cup cholesterol-free egg substitute
    2 tablespoons canola oil
    1 tablespoon grated fresh ginger
    8 ounces fat-free whipped topping

One 15-ounce can sweet potatoes in syrup, drained and mashed, equals about 1 cup.

1. Preheat oven to 350°F. Spray 13×9-inch baking pan with nonstick cooking spray.

2. Combine cake mix, water, sweet potatoes, egg whites, oil and ginger in large bowl; mix according to package directions. Pour batter into prepared pan.

3. Bake 32 to 34 minutes or until toothpick inserted into center comes out clean. Cool completely in pan on wire rack. Frost cake with whipped topping. Store covered in refrigerator. *Makes 18 servings*

Nutrients per Serving:
Calories: 174, **Calories from Fat:** 21%, **Total Fat:** 4g, **Saturated Fat:** 1g, **Cholesterol:** 0mg, **Sodium:** 217mg, **Carbohydrate:** 31g, **Fiber:** <1g, **Protein:** 2g

Dietary Exchanges: 2 Starch, ½ Fat

Sugar Cookies

1¾ cups all-purpose flour
¼ cup unprocessed bran
½ teaspoon baking soda
⅛ teaspoon salt
½ cup soft baking butter with canola oil
¼ cup sugar
¼ cup unsweetened applesauce
1 egg white
1 teaspoon vanilla
2 tablespoons plus ½ teaspoon red or green fine decorating sugar

1. Combine flour, bran, baking soda and salt in medium bowl.

2. Beat butter and sugar in large bowl with electric mixer at medium speed 1 minute or until creamy. Add applesauce, egg white and vanilla; beat at low speed just until blended. Beat at medium speed until smooth.

3. Gradually add flour mixture to butter mixture, beating at low speed until well blended. Divide dough in half. Shape each half into 11-inch log. Wrap in plastic wrap; freeze at least 1 hour.

4. Preheat oven to 350°F. Cut logs of dough crosswise into ¼-inch slices, turning log slightly after each slice to keep slices round. Dip half of one side of each cookie into decorating sugar. Place cookies, sugar side up, on cookie sheets.

5. Bake 6 to 8 minutes or until set. Cool on cookie sheets 2 minutes. Remove to wire racks to cool completely. *Makes 68 cookies*

Nutrients per Serving: 1 cookie
Calories: 30, **Calories from Fat:** 60%, **Total Fat:** 2g, **Saturated Fat:** <1g,
Cholesterol: 3mg, **Sodium:** 33mg, **Carbohydrate:** 4g, **Fiber:** <1g, **Protein:** <1g

Dietary Exchanges: ½ Starch

Sugar Cookies

Pumpkin Cake

3 cups all-purpose flour
2 teaspoons ground cinnamon
1 teaspoon baking soda
1 teaspoon ground nutmeg
1 teaspoon ground cloves
½ teaspoon baking powder
½ teaspoon salt
1 cup sucralose-sugar blend
½ cup canola oil
½ cup unsweetened applesauce
1 can (15 ounces) solid-pack pumpkin
¾ cup cholesterol-free egg substitute
Powdered sugar (optional)

1. Preheat oven to 325°F. Spray 13×9-inch baking pan with nonstick cooking spray. Combine flour, cinnamon, baking soda, nutmeg, cloves, baking powder and salt in medium bowl.

2. Beat sucralose-sugar blend, oil and applesauce in large bowl with electric mixer at medium speed 1 minute or until smooth. Beat in pumpkin and egg substitute until well blended.

3. Gradually add flour mixture to pumpkin mixture, beating just until blended. *Do not overmix.* Pour batter into prepared pan.

4. Bake 1 hour and 20 minutes or until toothpick inserted into center comes out clean. Cool completely in pan on wire rack. Cut into 24 pieces. Sprinkle with powdered sugar, if desired.

Makes 24 servings

Nutrients per Serving:
Calories: 150, **Calories from Fat:** 30%, **Total Fat:** 5g, **Saturated Fat:** <1g, **Cholesterol:** 0mg, **Sodium:** 127mg, **Carbohydrate:** 22g, **Fiber:** 1g, **Protein:** 3g

Dietary Exchanges: 1½ Starch, 1 Fat

Pumpkin Cake

Cranberry Phyllo Cheesecake Tarts

1 cup fresh or frozen cranberries
¼ cup sugar
2 tablespoons orange juice
1 teaspoon grated orange peel
¼ teaspoon ground allspice
6 sheets frozen phyllo dough, thawed
1 container (8 ounces) reduced-fat whipped cream cheese
8 ounces vanilla fat-free yogurt
1 tablespoon sugar or sugar substitute, divided
1 teaspoon vanilla

1. Preheat oven to 350°F. Combine cranberries, ¼ cup sugar, orange juice, orange peel and allspice in small saucepan; cook and stir over medium heat until berries pop and mixture thickens. Set aside to cool completely.

2. Lightly spray 12 standard (2½-inch) muffin cups with butter-flavored cooking spray. Cut phyllo sheets in half lengthwise, then crosswise into thirds. Spray 1 phyllo square lightly with cooking spray. Top with second square, slightly offsetting corners; spray lightly. Top with third square. Place stack of phyllo squares into one prepared muffin cup, pressing into bottom and up side of cup. Repeat with remaining phyllo squares. Bake 3 to 4 minutes or until golden. Cool completely in pan on wire rack.

3. Beat cream cheese, yogurt, 1 tablespoon sugar and vanilla in medium bowl with electric mixer until smooth. Divide mixture evenly among phyllo cups; top with cranberry mixture. *Makes 12 servings*

Nutrients per Serving: 1 tart
Calories: 92, **Calories from Fat:** 29%, **Total Fat:** 3g, **Saturated Fat:** 2g, **Cholesterol:** 11mg, **Sodium:** 143mg, **Carbohydrate:** 3g, **Fiber:** 1g, **Protein:** 3g

Dietary Exchanges: 1 Starch, ½ Fat

Cranberry Phyllo
Cheesecake Tart

Chocolate-Spice Bundt Cake with Orange Glaze

    1 package (about 18 ounces) devil's food cake mix
1⅓ cups water
    ¾ cup cholesterol-free egg substitute
    2 tablespoons canola oil
    1 tablespoon instant coffee granules
    1 tablespoon grated orange peel
    1 teaspoon ground cinnamon
    ½ cup orange juice
    1 teaspoon cornstarch

1. Preheat oven to 325°F. Spray nonstick bundt pan with nonstick cooking spray.

2. Beat cake mix, water, egg substitute, oil, coffee, orange peel and cinnamon in large bowl with electric mixer at medium speed until well blended. Pour batter into prepared pan.

3. Bake 35 to 37 minutes or until toothpick inserted near center comes out clean. Cool in pan on wire rack 10 minutes. Invert cake onto wire rack; cool completely.

4. Combine orange juice and cornstarch in small saucepan; stir until cornstarch is dissolved. Bring to a boil over medium-high heat; boil 1 minute or until thickened. Remove from heat; cool completely. Spoon glaze over cake.   *Makes 16 servings*

Variation: For deeper coffee flavor, add an additional 1 tablespoon coffee granules to cake batter. For deeper chocolate flavor, add 1 tablespoon unsweetened cocoa powder to cake batter.

Nutrients per Serving:
Calories: 164, Calories from Fat: 35%, Total Fat: 7g, Saturated Fat: 1g, Cholesterol: 0mg, Sodium: 289mg, Carbohydrate: 25g, Fiber: 1g, Protein: 3g

Dietary Exchanges: 1½ Starch, 1½ Fat

Chocolate-Spice Bundt Cake with Orange Glaze

Apple-Cranberry Crêpes

1 large baking apple, such as Gala or Jonathan, peeled, halved and cored
1 large tart apple, such as Granny Smith, peeled, halved and cored
¼ cup dried sweetened cranberries or cherries
2 tablespoons lemon juice
½ teaspoon plus ⅛ teaspoon ground cinnamon, divided
⅛ teaspoon ground nutmeg
⅛ teaspoon ground cloves or allspice
1 tablespoon diet margarine
¼ cup orange juice
1 tablespoon sugar substitute
¾ teaspoon cornstarch
¼ teaspoon almond extract
4 prepared crêpes
1 cup no-sugar-added low-fat vanilla ice cream

Slow Cooker Directions

1. Spray slow cooker with nonstick cooking spray. Cut each apple half into 3 wedges (making total of 12 wedges). Place apples, cranberries, lemon juice, ½ teaspoon cinnamon, nutmeg and cloves in slow cooker; toss to coat. Cover; cook on LOW 2 hours. Stir margarine into apple mixture just until melted.

2. Combine orange juice, sugar substitute, cornstarch and almond extract in small bowl; stir until cornstarch dissolves. Stir into apples; mix well. Cover; cook on HIGH 15 minutes to thicken sauce slightly.

3. Spoon apple mixture evenly down center of each crêpe. Fold edges over filling; place crêpes, seam side down, on plates. Sprinkle with remaining ⅛ teaspoon cinnamon. Heat filled crêpes in microwave, if desired. Serve with ice cream. *Makes 4 servings*

Nutrients per Serving: 1 crêpe with 3 apple wedges, 1 tablespoon sauce and ¼ cup ice cream
Calories: 235, **Calories from Fat:** 33%, **Total Fat:** 9g, **Saturated Fat:** 2g, **Cholesterol:** 101mg, **Sodium:** 221mg, **Carbohydrate:** 34g, **Fiber:** 3g, **Protein:** 6g

Dietary Exchanges: 1 Fruit, 1 Starch, 2 Fat

Apple-Cranberry Crêpes

Flourless Chocolate Cake

3 squares (1 ounce each) semisweet chocolate, cut into large pieces
3 tablespoons margarine
1 tablespoon espresso powder or instant coffee granules
2 tablespoons hot water
4 eggs, separated
2 egg whites
⅔ cup sugar, divided
3 tablespoons unsweetened cocoa powder, sifted
1 teaspoon vanilla
½ teaspoon salt
   Fat-free whipped topping and fresh raspberries (optional)

1. Preheat oven to 300°F. Grease 9-inch springform pan; line bottom of pan with parchment paper.

2. Place chocolate and margarine in small heavy saucepan; heat over low heat, stirring frequently, just until melted. Remove from heat; set aside to cool. Dissolve espresso powder in hot water in small bowl.

3. Place 6 egg whites in large bowl. Beat egg yolks in medium bowl with electric mixer at high speed about 5 minutes or until pale yellow in color. Add ⅓ cup sugar; beat 4 minutes or until mixture falls in ribbons from beaters. Slowly beat in melted chocolate mixture and espresso mixture at low speed just until blended. Beat in cocoa and vanilla just until blended.

4. Add salt to egg whites; beat at high speed 2 minutes or until soft peaksform. Beat in remaining ⅓ cup sugar until stiff peaks form. Stir spoonful of egg whites into chocolate mixture. Fold chocolate mixture into egg whites until almost blended. Spoon batter into prepared pan.

continued on page 136

Flourless Chocolate Cake

Flourless Chocolate Cake, continued

5. Bake 1 hour or until cake begins to pull away from side of pan. Cool in pan on wire rack 10 minutes. Run thin spatula around edge of cake; carefully remove side of pan. Cool completely.

6. Invert cake onto serving plate; remove bottom of pan and paper. Cover and refrigerate at least 4 hours. Serve chilled with whipped topping and raspberries, if desired.   ***Makes 10 servings***

Tip: Before beating the egg whites, make sure that your bowl and beaters are clean and dry. Any grease or yolk that is present will decrease the volume of the egg whites.

Nutrients per Serving:
Calories: 190, **Calories from Fat:** 38%, **Total Fat:** 8g, **Saturated Fat:** 3g, **Cholesterol:** 85mg, **Sodium:** 240mg, **Carbohydrate:** 26g, **Fiber:** 1g, **Protein:** 4g

Dietary Exchanges: 1½ Starch, 1 Fat

Peach-Cranberry Cobbler with Corn Bread Biscuits

    1 package (16 ounces) frozen unsweetened sliced peaches, thawed
    1 cup fresh or frozen cranberries or raspberries
    ⅓ cup orange juice
    ¼ cup packed brown sugar
    2 tablespoons plus ⅓ cup all-purpose flour, divided
    ⅛ teaspoon ground allspice
    3 tablespoons yellow cornmeal
    1 tablespoon granulated sugar
    1 teaspoon baking powder
    ¼ teaspoon salt
    2 tablespoons cold butter
    1 egg
    3 tablespoons fat-free (skim) milk

1. Preheat oven to 400°F. Combine peaches, cranberries and orange juice in large bowl. Combine brown sugar, 2 tablespoons flour and allspice in small bowl; stir into peach mixture. Spoon about ½ cup peach mixture into each of 6 (8-ounce) custard cups or ramekins.

2. For biscuits, combine remaining ⅓ cup flour, cornmeal, granulated sugar, baking powder and salt in medium bowl. Cut in butter with 2 knives or pastry blender until mixture resembles coarse crumbs. Whisk egg and milk in small bowl. Stir egg mixture into flour mixture with fork just until moistened. Spoon biscuit topping evenly over peach mixture.

3. Bake 20 to 25 minutes or until toothpick inserted into topping comes out clean. *Makes 6 servings*

Nutrients per Serving: 1 cobbler
Calories: 184, **Calories from Fat:** 24%, **Total Fat:** 5g, **Saturated Fat:** 3g, **Cholesterol:** 46mg, **Sodium:** 226mg, **Carbohydrate:** 33g, **Fiber:** 3g, **Protein:** 3g

Dietary Exchanges: 1 Starch, 1 Fat

Allspice is not a mixture of spices but it does taste like a combination of cinnamon, nutmeg and cloves. Allspice is available both whole and ground, and like other spices, it should be stored in a cool dark place.

Maple-Sweet Potato Cheesecake Pies

1 package (8 ounces) reduced-fat cream cheese, softened
½ cup vanilla sugar-free fat-free yogurt
1 can (16 ounces) sweet potatoes, drained and mashed (see Tip)
½ cup pure maple syrup
1 teaspoon vanilla
½ teaspoon ground cinnamon
¼ teaspoon ground cloves
1 egg
1 egg white
12 mini graham cracker crusts
12 pecan halves

1. Preheat oven to 350°F. Beat cream cheese in medium bowl with electric mixer at medium speed until creamy. Beat in yogurt until smooth. Beat in mashed sweet potatoes, syrup, vanilla, cinnamon and cloves until smooth. Beat in egg and egg white until combined.

2. Spoon sweet potato mixture evenly into crusts (about ⅓ cup per crust). Top each with pecan half. Place filled crusts on large baking sheet.

3. Bake 30 to 35 minutes or until set and knife inserted into centers comes out clean. Cool on wire rack 1 hour. Refrigerate before serving.

Makes 12 servings

Tip: Mashing sweet potatoes by hand produces pie filling with a somewhat coarse texture. For a smoother texture, process sweet potatoes in a food processor until smooth.

Variation: Pour sweet potato mixture into 9-inch graham cracker crust. Bake 40 to 45 minutes.

Nutrients per Serving: 1 pie
Calories: 257, **Calories from Fat:** 37%, **Total Fat:** 10g, **Saturated Fat:** 4g,
Cholesterol: 32mg, **Sodium:** 234mg, **Carbohydrate:** 35g, **Fiber:** 2g, **Protein:** 4g

Dietary Exchanges: 2½ Starch, 2 Fat

*Maple-Sweet Potato
Cheesecake Pie*

Pumpkin Custard

1 can (15 ounces) solid-pack pumpkin
1 teaspoon pumpkin pie spice
⅛ teaspoon salt
¾ cup fat-free evaporated milk
3 eggs *or* ¾ cup cholesterol-free egg substitute
¼ cup packed dark brown sugar
2 tablespoons chopped dried cherries
2 tablespoons low-fat granola
4 cups boiling water

1. Preheat oven to 350°F. Lightly spray 6 (6-ounce) custard cups with nonstick cooking spray. Place cups in 13×9-inch baking pan. Stir pumpkin, pumpkin pie spice and salt in medium bowl until blended.

2. Heat milk in small saucepan until steaming but not boiling. Meanwhile, whisk eggs and sugar in large bowl until smooth. Gradually whisk hot milk into egg mixture. Whisk in pumpkin mixture until blended. Spoon custard evenly into prepared cups; sprinkle with cherries and granola.

3. Place baking pan in oven; pour boiling water into pan until water reaches halfway up sides of custard cups.

4. Bake 25 to 30 minutes or until knife inserted into centers comes out clean. Remove cups to wire rack. Serve custard warm or chilled.

Makes 6 servings

Nutrients per Serving: 1 custard
Calories: 141, **Calories from Fat:** 18%, **Total Fat:** 3g, **Saturated Fat:** <1g, **Cholesterol:** 107mg, **Sodium:** 134mg, **Carbohydrate:** 24g, **Fiber:** 2g, **Protein:** 7g

Dietary Exchanges: 1½ Starch, ½ Fat

Nutritional Analysis for Recipes in this Cookbook

The nutritional calculations for each recipe were based on the following:

• Each analysis is based on a single serving.

• Optional ingredients and garnishes were not included.

• If a range is given for an ingredient, the lesser amount was used. If an ingredient is presented with an option (e.g., 2 cups hot cooked rice or noodles), the first item listed was the one used.

• In photographs, extra foods shown on the same serving plate with the featured recipe were not included.

• Meats were trimmed of all visible fat. Cooked rice, pasta and noodles were prepared without added salt and fat.

• Dietary exchanges listed are based on the Exchange Lists for Meal Planning, developed by the American Diabetes Association, Inc., and the American Dietetic Association.

Metric Conversion Chart

VOLUME MEASUREMENTS (dry)

⅛ teaspoon = 0.5 mL
¼ teaspoon = 1 mL
½ teaspoon = 2 mL
¾ teaspoon = 4 mL
1 teaspoon = 5 mL
1 tablespoon = 15 mL
2 tablespoons = 30 mL
¼ cup = 60 mL
⅓ cup = 75 mL
½ cup = 125 mL
⅔ cup = 150 mL
¾ cup = 175 mL
1 cup = 250 mL
2 cups = 1 pint = 500 mL
3 cups = 750 mL
4 cups = 1 quart = 1 L

VOLUME MEASUREMENTS (fluid)

1 fluid ounce (2 tablespoons) = 30 mL
4 fluid ounces (½ cup) = 125 mL
8 fluid ounces (1 cup) = 250 mL
12 fluid ounces (1½ cups) = 375 mL
16 fluid ounces (2 cups) = 500 mL

WEIGHTS (mass)

½ ounce = 15 g
1 ounce = 30 g
3 ounces = 90 g
4 ounces = 120 g
8 ounces = 225 g
10 ounces = 285 g
12 ounces = 360 g
16 ounces = 1 pound = 450 g

DIMENSIONS

1/16 inch = 2 mm
⅛ inch = 3 mm
¼ inch = 6 mm
½ inch = 1.5 cm
¾ inch = 2 cm
1 inch = 2.5 cm

OVEN TEMPERATURES

250°F = 120°C
275°F = 140°C
300°F = 150°C
325°F = 160°C
350°F = 180°C
375°F = 190°C
400°F = 200°C
425°F = 220°C
450°F = 230°C

BAKING PAN SIZES

Utensil	Size in Inches/Quarts	Metric Volume	Size in Centimeters
Baking or Cake Pan (square or rectangular)	8×8×2	2 L	20×20×5
	9×9×2	2.5 L	23×23×5
	12×8×2	3 L	30×20×5
	13×9×2	3.5 L	33×23×5
Loaf Pan	8×4×3	1.5 L	20×10×7
	9×5×3	2 L	23×13×7
Round Layer Cake Pan	8×1½	1.2 L	20×4
	9×1½	1.5 L	23×4
Pie Plate	8×1¼	750 mL	20×3
	9×1¼	1 L	23×3
Baking Dish or Casserole	1 quart	1 L	—
	1½ quart	1.5 L	—
	2 quart	2 L	—